MW00423028

Flavor Math

A guide to understanding and creating delicious flavor combinations

Contents

This book is structured into 3 big main parts. First, you have the scientific and theoretical culinary background of taste and flavors to help you understand how to balance your dishes. Second, you have the more common, tried and trusted flavor combinations. Thirdly, you have the more daring and truly exciting flavor combinations. Obviously, there are some other parts structured around them as well. You can find the overview of all parts below.

Overview of all parts in the book

Foreword

Overview of all parts in the book

I started writing this book because I wanted to understand flavor better myself. Ever since I stumbled upon the chemical processes that influence which flavors go well together I was hooked on the topic! The result is this book that is meant to spark your creativity while giving you better knowledge why certain combinations just work better than others.

There are some traditional flavor combinations that are tried and trusted by most people and then there are the big unknown paths only a few people dare to walk. Off the beaten track, however, you can find incredible combinations you would have never thought of! Inspired by the greatest chefs and restaurants around the world this book will provide you with 66 of the best combinations from both worlds - the known and familiar as well as the strange but extra-ordinary.

By experimenting with ingredients, you develop your palate and build your personal taste memory. With taste memory, you will be able create taste combinations in your head rather than in the pan. This saves you time, money and effort in the long run. An extensive memory unfortunately takes years and years to develop. If you understand taste elements however, you will be quickly able to perfectly balance flavors and substitute ingredients confidently.

This book will be your little cheat book with tried and trusted combinations. Combinations that are known to work because the individual elements fit together like a glove. There is no reason to reinvent the wheel time and time again! You can build on the experience of countless chefs, scientists and food writers making it easy for you to wow your guests!

I sincerely hope you enjoy the flavor combinations in this book and can delight your friends and family with them. Hopefully it also helps to nudge you to becoming a more creative and confident cook in the long run so you can hustle up your own extraordinary flavor combinations with ease.

Johnny

Owner of www.InJohnnysKitchen.com

and author of the cookbook "In Johnny's Kitchen

Various small little fruit tarts
Photo by Brooke Lark

What are taste and flavor to begin with?

Tasting deliciousness

The taste buds on your tongue can only differentiate between five different tastes: Sweet, salty, sour, bitter and umami. Though most people are obviously familiar with the first four tastes "umami" is still not that known. The name was coined in Japan and roughly translates to "pleasant savory taste".

Umami is closely related to glutamate and can be found naturally in tomatoes, mushrooms, cheese as well as in a lot of smoked and fermented foods. There is however also the artificial way which is usually adding MSG to enhance the flavor of the dish.

Tasting deliciousness

Taste is only one part of the final flavor. The other two big factors are aroma and mouthfeel. Aroma – the smell of a food - accounts for about 80% of the flavor. So, your nose does a better job of making you appreciate a dish than the actual taste buds on your tongue. That is also the reason why eating something with your nose pinched keeps you from tasting a lot of the dish.

Better make sure your food is fragrant and smells pleasant. Use fresh herbs and aromatic spices to ensure the dish is at its best!

Next to aroma, the mouthfeel of a dish is very important as well. Your mouth will notice the richness, crunchiness and of course the temperature. Richness comes primarily from that slightly fatty coating feeling on your tongue. Think of having rich broth or ice cream in your mouth. This is opposite to the crisp astringent feeling that you would get from a zingy little salad or biting into a slice of lemon.

Texture is very important as well as it makes a dish more interesting. Play with soft and crunchy elements and cut vegetables at an angle into different shapes. A dish is more pleasant to eat if every bite just brings a little bit extra with it.

The temperature of a dish also plays a big role in the amount of flavor that you perceive. Hot days call for colder dishes with cooling cucumber, whereas cold winter nights make you crave those piquant and warming stews. Certain ingredients like mint or red pepper can trick your tongue in thinking that a dish is cooler or hotter than it actually is.

Make sure taste, aroma, mouthfeel and temperate are all balanced for the best experience.

The proper way to balancing flavors

Balancing flavor

What determines the difference between a mediocre and a great dish? The perfect balance of flavor! By learning how to balance your dishes just a little bit better, you will make great steps towards becoming a better cook!

Sweet and sour are two opposite taste extremes, the same is true for salty and bitter. Rich and often umami heavy food is the polar opposite of crisp and light dishes. On this page you will find a little guide what to do if the flavor of a dish is a little off.

Too sweet? Add sour! Balance it out with a squeeze of lemon, a splash of vinegar or some tart fruit.

Too sour? More sweetness! Use some sugar, honey, sweet tropical fruit or roasted vegetables.

Too salty? Use bitter ingredients! Unsweetened chocolate, coffee, beer, mustard but also spinach, brussels sprouts and broccoli deliver a little kick of bitterness.

Too bitter? Salt does the trick! Use regular salt, salted nuts, soy sauce, or ingredients like anchovies and artichokes.

Too rich? Cut the richness with some zing! Use tangy citrus fruits like lime and lemon or sour condiments like sauerkraut, kimchi or gherkins.

Not rich enough? Add fat and umami! Cream, butter and oil add fatty richness, while seared red meats, mushrooms, cheese and fermented foods like fish sauce add savory richness.

Of course, the best way of making sure your dish tastes perfect is taste it, taste it, and taste it again. By tasting several times during the cooking process, you can make sure your dish hits all the right notes!

There are various different models out there on how to balance out flavor. The sketch on the next page is my little model of the world. I use this little tool to make sure my dishes are balanced well.

Johnny's visual model to balancing flavors

Three dimensions to balance

- sweet vs. sour
- salty vs. bitter
- rich vs. crisp

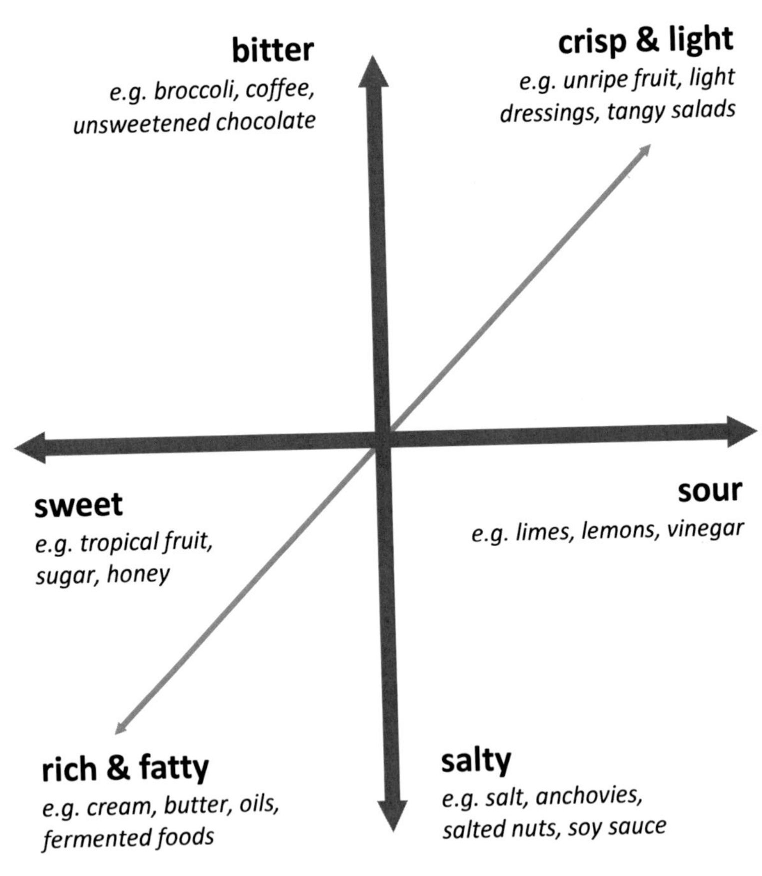

The magic of the sweet and the savory

Fat, sugar and salt - the sex lube of our culinary generation

"When in doubt, use a touch of fat, sugar and salt. These ingredients have become the sex lube of our culinary generation. It's kind of awful. But I'm not entirely opposed to the sugar-fat-salt trick; I just think it needs to be used very, very prudently"

Andrew Zimmern

A magic formula because we still have monkey brains

We are all evolutionary simply hardwired to love this combination. Back in the past, these three distinct taste elements were almost a guarantee for energy and filling nutrition that would sustain us in the times of need to come.

Whenever a dish tastes bland, add a dash of sugar, a sprinkle of salt and a generous amount of butter - or simply cut out the middle man and add bacon! Voilà, your dish tastes better than ever before! The reason is that your monkey brain just tells your body "yes, this is exactly what we should be eating so we won't starve to death in the near future".

Andrew Zimmern is one of my biggest inspirations when it comes to culinary adventures. When I first read his quote, I felt a little guilty! I use this little cheap shortcut quite often without even realizing it.

The combination of rich fatty and salty umami flavor, combined with a hint of sweetness always appealed to me! I just love the combination of sweet and savory in all kinds of dishes: Pineapple on a burger, baked peaches with cheese and bacon, and of course a nice cheese platter with a variety of jams.

In my little flavor model, you can find this "magical sweet spot" in the bottom left. If you properly want to impress your guest, this is probably your best chance and easiest way of doing it!

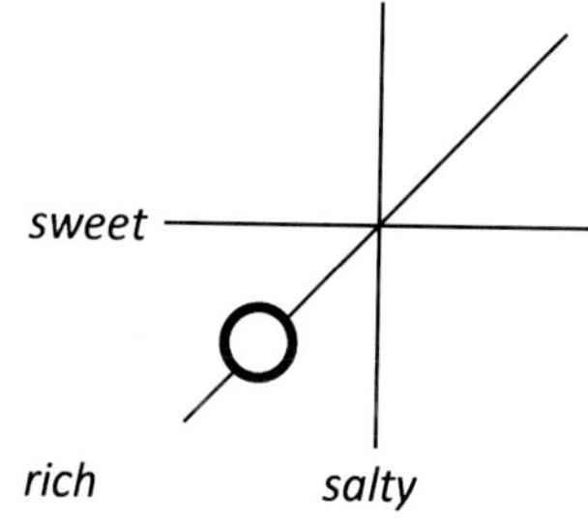

The art and science of substitution

As soon as you understand why the combinations work well together you can come up with countless different recipes and dishes. Even better, many ingredients can be substituted with related ingredients that share a similar flavor profile. This leaves you with almost endless possibilities.

There is a scientific approach to this that is based on the notion that ingredients with similar chemical build-up share similar flavor compounds. Ergo, these two ingredients therefore can also be rather easily substituted for another, while still delivering you with a similar result in terms of flavor.

Whole books have been written about food pairings and substitutions, while online communities and artificial intelligences have been built around it. Naming all these substitutions would definitely blow-up the scope of this book in particular. If you are interested in these I can recommend the following books and websites on the right.

The books named underneath are extensive reference works which a lot of the combinations in this book are based on. The books are based on years and years of research by the authors. If you want to dig deeper into the science of flavor combinations I can highly recommend buying them.

Books:

Karen Page & Andrew Dornenburg - Flavour bible

Karen Page & Andrew Dornenburg - Culinary artistry

Angelique Schmeink – Smaakvrienden (Dutch)

Websites:

www.informationisbeautiful.net/visualizations/taste-buds

Visualization of several dominant flavor combinations.

www.chefwatson.com

IBM's own artificial intelligence makes it easy for you to create your own spectacular flavor combinations. Draft recipes included!

www.foodpairing.com

A whole business build around combinations and pairings of flavors started by former Michelin star chef Peter Coucquyt

"I feel a recipe is only a theme, which an intelligent cook can play each time with a variation"

Madame Jehane Benoit

Books about flavors and combinations
Photo by Jean-Marie Leufkens

How to read this book

The different elements on each page

All pages in this book are structured the same way. This page gives you a quick guide on how to read them. On top of the page you will find the ***ingredients*** featured in the combination. Under the photos you will find an explanation ***why*** the combinations work and ***how*** to marry the flavors. At the bottom there is some ***inspiration*** for actual dishes. The ***scale*** helps you to identify how crazy the combination is. In the top right corner you can find the unique ***number*** of the combination. This makes it easier for you to remember and find them if you are looking for a specific number.

Understand the why & the how

On each page you will find the combination of 2-3 ingredients. For each combination there is a description on the left side ***why*** the combination works from a flavor point of view. By understanding the why you can easily come up with your own combinations. Next to *why* you will find a general description ***how*** to combine the flavors into a dish. Some of the descriptions are more specific than others. It all depends on the ingredients.

At the bottom of the page you will find 3 actual suggestions of dishes you could make. These ***inspirations*** are not full recipes but you will be easily able to find full descriptive recipes as soon as you type in the suggestions into for example google.

Use the 'weirdness' scale

To give you an idea on how weird I personally would rate the flavor combinations I added a little ***scale*** for easy reference.

If you are somewhat hesitant or conservative you might want to stick with the combinations that have a rating of 1 or 2.

For the more daring chefs I strongly advise you to give the combinations with a rating of 3 and 4 a go. Trust me, all combinations are tried and trusted by myself - otherwise I would not feature them here.

This is how the pages are build up

Combination #

Ingredient 1 + Ingredient 2

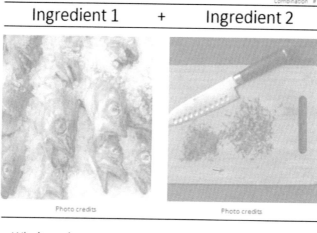

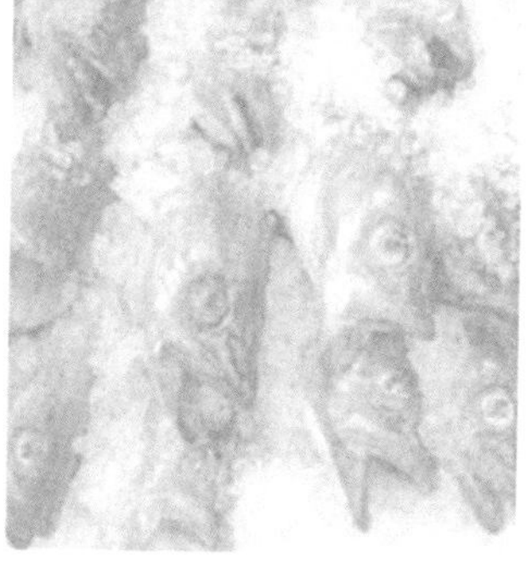

Photo credits

Photo credits

Why it works

How to prepare

Inspiration for dishes

Page #

A note on the photography in this book

Purely illustration? Nope!

For the various ingredients in this book there are pictures included. This serves actually 3 purposes:

1. It makes it easy for you to see at first glance what ingredients are used because you are obviously familiar how the different foods look like. If you were not familiar with it - now you know what to look for!

2. I wanted to feature some great but mostly unknown food photographers in this book! While writing my first cookbook "In Johnny's Kitchen" I taught myself the basics on how to take pictures of food. Food photography is an artform in itself and takes years and years to master. There are a lot of talented professionals and amateurs alike our there that take the most beautiful and mouth-watering pictures of delicious dishes and ingredients. In this book you can find a lot of talented individuals that deserve their space in the spotlight.

3. But then again at the very end of the day, photos simply also make the book look more pretty and delicious, right?

Photo credits

I truly believe credit should be given where credit is due. Even though all pictures used in this book are freely available online if not mentioned otherwise, their makers truly deserve the credit.

Below each picture you will find the author of the picture either with their full name or their online pseudonym. If you would like to get in touch with them then just type in their name into google and contact them.

Most photos came from www.unsplash.com, the world's most generous community of photographers. Next to that, some other websites where used as well.

The full index of the websites can be found on page 100.

Photos on the right page are from:

- *Apple – Roberta Sorge*
- *Chocolate – Michal Grosicki*
- *Chicken – Jairo Alzate*
- *Mint – Dave Meier*

33 classic, tried and trusted combinations

This chapter of the book features more classic flavor combinations. Think of Tomato & Basil, Ham & Cheese, or Honey & Mustard! They are time-honored classics and marriages made in heaven. You might already know some of these and have even prepared dishes with them in the past. For each combination you can read why they work and might still get some extra inspiration from the suggested dishes mentioned. Even if you have not heard of a combination before, you will probably think:

"Yeah, that kinda makes sense! Why didn't I think of this before?"

The classic combination: Tomato and Basil
Photo by Dennis Klein

Anchovies + Parsley

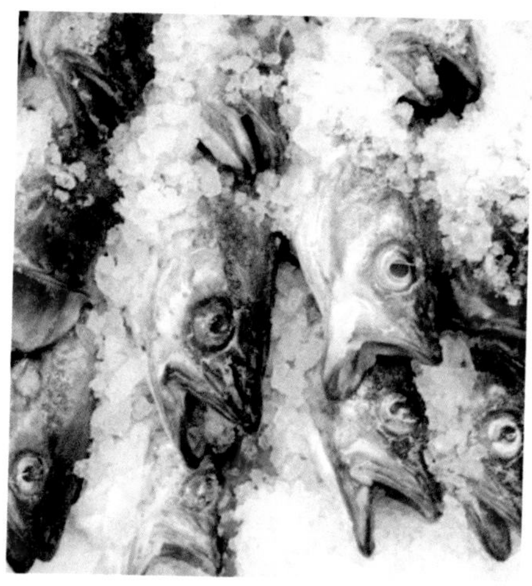

Photo by Jorge Gonzalez

Photo by Krzysztof Puszczyński

Why it works

The herbaciousness of the parsley complements the fatty and rich flavor of the anchovies, while the salt of the fish brings out the grassy and slightly lemony flavor of the parsley even more.

How to prepare

Finely chop the two together into a rough pesto-like paste (gremolata). It works perfectly as light fresh topping for Mediterranean fish or meat dishes. Use the paste sparingly though. You do not want to overpower the hero of your dish.

Inspiration for dishes

- As topping for grilled meat, fish or vegetables
- Toss pasta with chopped anchovies, parsley, olives and pine nuts
- Make a tabbouleh-like salad with couscous, chunks of anchovies, tomatoes, spring onions and lots of parsley

Fish sauce + Lime juice + Brown sugar

Photo by Caroline Attwood

Photo by Hoach Le Dinh

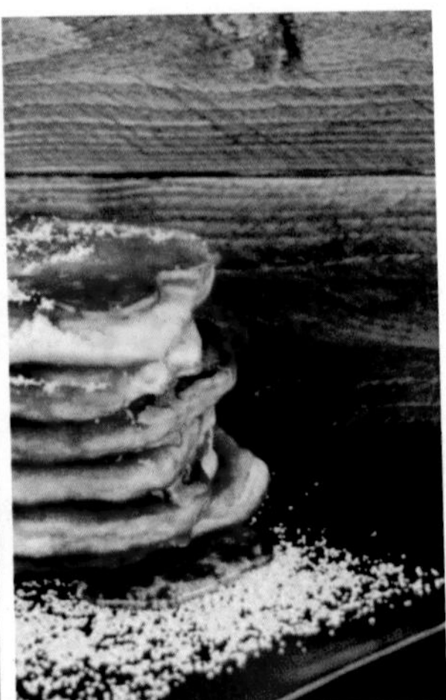
Photo by Jean-Marie Leufkens

Why it works

A classical Thai combination. The salty fish sauce is balanced out by the sweetness of the brown sugar while the lime juice cuts through the sweet and salty. You get a fresh and rich taste that immediately transfers you to the shores of Thailand.

No brainer  Weird

How to prepare

Perfect as a dressing for noodles or salads. Add some red pepper flakes for some extra kick! It works great in fresh salads or with tangy fruits.

Inspiration for dishes

- Pad Thai: Toss rice noodles with the mixture, some veggies and crushed peanuts
- Make a Thai-inspired cucumber salad
- Mix shredded mango, green papaya or cabbage with the mixture and some cilantro

Ginger + Garlic + Spring onion

Photo by Dominik Martin

Photo by Fireskystudios.com

Photo by Congerdesign

Why it works

The sharp fresh notes of the ginger counters the intense and pungent flavor of the garlic. Both have a spiciness to them that go really well together. Combined with the fresh crunch of spring onions you end up with a trio that will kickstart your taste buds.

No brainer   Weird

How to prepare

It's the perfect base for all Asian stir-fries. Add the spring onion in the last step of your cooking to ensure they remain crunchy fresh and deliver an extra texture contrast to the dish.

Inspiration for dishes

- Ground pork fried with ginger, garlic, eggplant and chili sauce
- Chicken fried with shallots, ginger, garlic and oyster sauce
- Sliced beef stir fried with ginger, garlic and bell peppers

Bacon + Maple syrup

Photo by Andrew Rdley

Photo by Nabil Boulaka

Why it works

This combination embodies the magical trifection of fat, sugar and salt. The rich fattiness of the bacon is complemented by the smooth silky texture of the maple syrup. This combination just oozes decadence.

How to prepare

Bake bacon to crispy perfection and slather it with the delicious syrup. This works perfectly with pancakes, but even more as an adventurous topping for cupcakes.

Inspiration for dishes

- Cupcake topped with caramelized crispy bacon bits
- Bacon encased pancake batter drizzled with syrup
- Burger with caramelized onions, bacon and a drizzle of syrup

Cumin + Oregano + Chipotle pepper

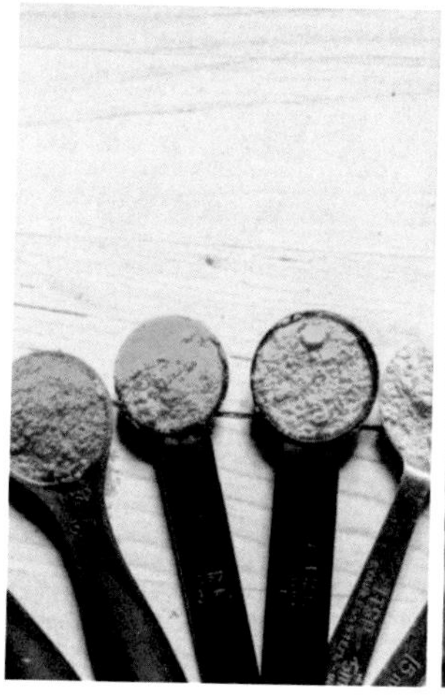
Photo by Beth Teutschmann

Photo by Chuttersnap

Photo by Coyot

Why it works

The warm spicy curry like taste of the cumin is contrasted by the floral lightly bitter lemony taste of the oregano. The heat and smokiness of the chipotle pepper rounds this off into a deep and complex mix of flavors.

No brainer ■ □ □ □ Weird

How to prepare

This combination is typical for the Mexican cuisine and works well with grilled meat and chicken. Use it for example as flavor basis for your taco fillings. It can also be used in Middle Eastern-style lentil soup.

Inspiration for dishes

- Chicken marinated in the mix with some olive oil and then grill it
- Slow cooked pork shredded as taco filling
- Vegetarian stir-fry with bell pepper, corn and tomatoes

Honey + Mustard

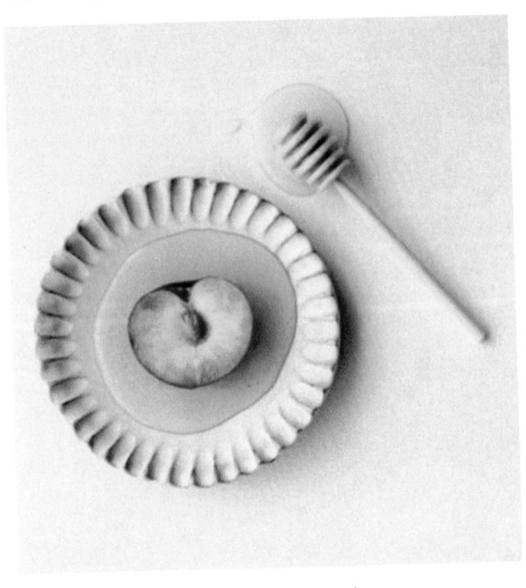

Photo by Krista McPhee

Photo by Jay Wennington

Why it works

Lightly sweet but biting sharp flavor of the mustard is mellowed out by the smooth creaminess of the honey. The two flavor extremes of pungent sharpness and indulgent sweetness melt together into a balanced symphony.

No brainer  Weird

How to prepare

Combine mustard (preferably wholegrain or Dijon mustard) with honey and stir until they come together. This mixture can be used as topping as well as dressing or even marinade for all kinds of dishes.

Inspiration for dishes

- Dressing for salad with lettuce greens
- Drizzle over black olives and cheese
- As dipping sauce for chicken wings or even boiled sausage

Cilantro + Lime

Photo by Syd Wachs

Photo by Luke Besley

Why it works

Cilantro's fresh and slightly zingy taste works perfectly well with the zingy taste of lime. The two complement each other well and can lighten up a lot of your dishes.

No brainer  Weird

How to prepare

Use cilantro at the end of your cooking in Asian dishes or as garnish for your Mexican delights. The two work beautiful as marinade too. Some people (especially in the West) can't stand the taste of cilantro at all, because they perceive it as soapy. Use small amounts initially and let guest take seconds if they want more.

Inspiration for dishes

- As marinade with jalapenos for meat
- As finishing touch in Thai salads and green curries, or as Vietnamese summer rolls
- Drizzle tacos with a squirt of lime juice and top with chopped cilantro

Mushrooms + Tarragon + Creamy dairy

Photo by Nick Grappone

Photo by Thomas Rehehauser

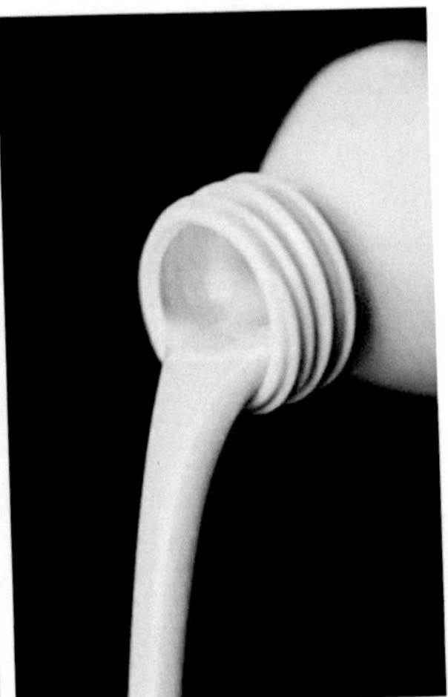

Photo by Tookapic

Why it works

Mushrooms just love creamy sauces in general and the slightly sweet liquorish taste of tarragon melts into the subtle flavor of the mushrooms.

How to prepare

The combination is a regular staple for French cuisine and works particularly well with fish and poultry.

Inspiration for dishes

- Vegetarian quiche with zucchini and asparagus
- Chicken with mushroom and cream sauce
- Oven-baked salmon with a mushroom and cream sauce

Prosciutto + Melon

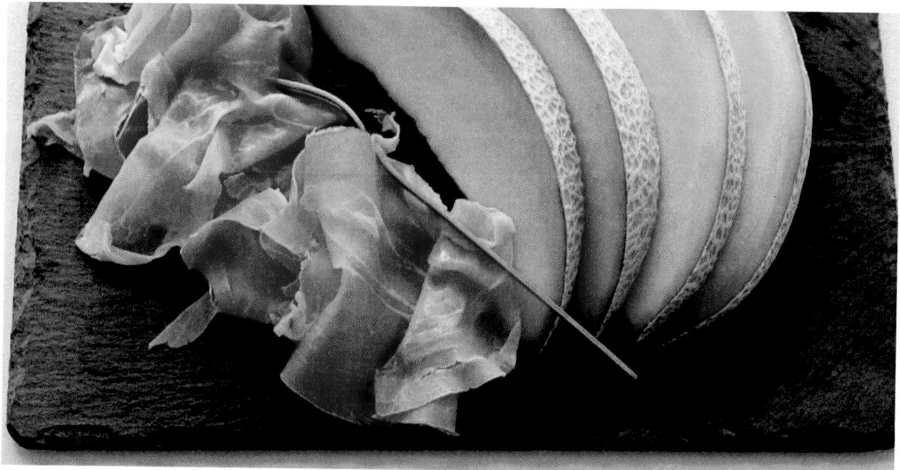

Photo by Erbs55

Why it works

No brainer  Weird

The salty and rich prosciutto offsets and complements the (sometimes overly) sweet taste of the melon. This combination of sweet and savory is definitely a winning combination.

How to prepare

The easiest way to marry the flavor is to simply wrap the melon with the prosciutto. This can be done with bite-size pieces but also with whole skin-off slices of melon.

Inspiration for dishes

- As canapé with bite-size melon pieces wrapped in ham on a small blini pancake
- Melon salad with bits of crispy baked prosciutto
- Prosciutto wrapped melon pieces on a cheese platter

Peach caprese salad with buffalo mozzare
Photo by Jean-Marie Leufkens

Tomato + Basil

Photo by Dennis Klein

Why it works

Sweet tomatoes just love the slightly peppery intense rich flavor of basil! No wonder you find this combination in so many Italian dishes.

How to prepare

The combination of tomato and basil works well fresh as well as in cooked dishes. Cooked rich tomato sauce profits from the taste of fresh basil just like raw tomatoes in a salad. Always go for fresh basil with its intoxicating smell and skipped the tasteless dried herbs!

Inspiration for dishes

- Prawns in garlic white wine sauce with cherry tomatoes and lots of basil
- As caprese salad: Alternating slices of tomato and mozzarella, drizzled with olive oil and sprinkled with torn basil
- Pasta with oven-roasted tomatoes, fresh basil pesto and shaved parmesan cheese

Watermelon + Feta + Mint

Photo by Neha Deshmukh

Photo by Anita Peeples

Photo by Dave Meier

No brainer  Weird

Why it works

The rich slightly tangy taste of the feta is complemented by the sweetness of the watermelon. A touch of mint gives a refreshing contrast that partly cleanses your pallet and makes you want to take another bite, and another, and another...

How to prepare

Cube watermelon and feta, then sprinkle them with some torn mint for a fresh summery salad. You can even quickly grill or broil your watermelon covered with feta to end up with some melted gooey cheese.

Inspiration for dishes

- As a salad with either cubed or crumbled feta, thinly sliced red onion and a glug of olive oil
- Sliced watermelon with crumbled feta quickly broiled until melted
- Taco topping: Quick salsa with diced watermelon, sprinkled with feta and mint

Watermelon, feta and mint salad
Photo by Jean-Marie Leufkens

Yoghurt + Cucumber + Dill

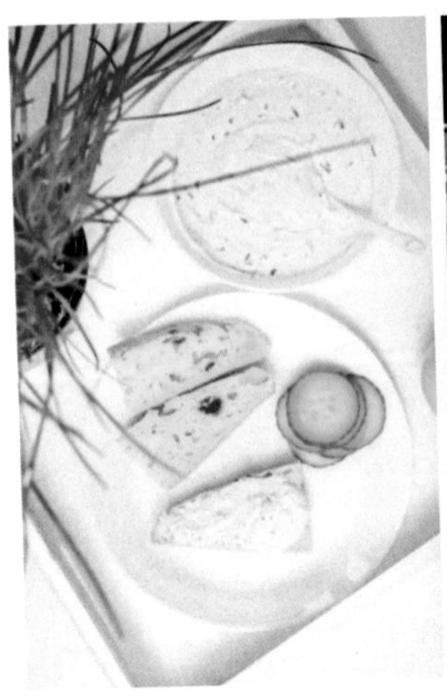
Photo by Katerina Pavlickova

Photo by Jonathan Pielmayer

Photo by Piotr Lohunko

No brainer | Weird

Why it works

The mellow taste of the cucumber pairs well with the slightly tanginess of the yoghurt, while the dill gives a refreshing and aromatic finish.

How to prepare

Especially when the 3 ingredients are paired with garlic they create an irresistible fresh sauce that is known as tzatziki in the Greece and Turkish cuisine. It works very well with grilled fish and meats. Drained thick high-fat yoghurt works best. The Bulgarian kitchen uses this combination in a salad they call 'snezanka'.

Inspiration for dishes

- As dipping sauce with grated or finely diced de-seeded cucumber
- Blinis or small latkes with smoked salmon, a dollop of thick yoghurt piled with diced cucumber and dill
- Fresh cold gazpacho soup with a swirl of yoghurt

Broccoli + Garlic

Photo by Joanna Kosinska

Photo by Fireskystudios.com

Why it works

The nutrition-packed but slightly bitter tasting broccoli profits from the rich pungent taste of garlic. Especially for the people that do not particularly like the taste of broccoli, this combination can be a good way to familiarize them with the healthy green.

No brainer ■ □ □ □ Weird

How to prepare

No matter if the broccoli is cooked, stir-fried, roasted or pureed, garlic can be used in every cooking technique along the way. A touch of chili can give some nice spiciness to the combo, while a squirt of lime can lift up the dish.

Inspiration for dishes

- As a salad with oven roasted broccoli and finely sliced sautéed garlic and chili flakes
- Broccoli soup with a touch of garlic and a swirl of crème fraiche
- Stir-fried chicken and broccoli with garlic in oyster sauce

Banana + Chocolate

Photo by Ashwin Vaswani

Photo by Jennifer Pallian

Why it works

The sweet taste of banana gets and extra level of indulgence with the creamy richness of the chocolate. The two just basically melt together into a rich luxurious combination.

How to prepare

Melted chocolate works best to cover the banana, but sprinkles of shaved chocolate will work just as well to finish off a delicious banana dessert or ice cream. Mashed banana and melted chocolate make for an excellent filling for grilled sandwiches or French toast.

Inspiration for dishes

- Banana ice cream with chocolate sprinkles or chocolate-rum sauce
- Pancakes topped with sliced banana and chocolate syrup
- Deep-fried banana in tempura batter drizzled with chocolate sauce

Triple chocolate ice cream with warm banana, chocolate and rum sauce
Photo by Jean-Marie Leufkens

Brussels sprouts + Bacon

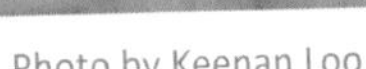
Photo by Keenan Loo

Photo by Andrew Ridley

Why it works

No brainer  Weird

The bitterness of Brussels sprouts can be overwhelming for some and a touch of bacon can offset the taste even for the most determined Brussels sprouts haters. The salty richness of the bacon complements and contrasts the strong and bitter taste of the Brussels sprouts.

How to prepare

Render bacon in a skilled, remove and stir-fry the sprouts in the bacon fat. Oven-roasted sprouts profit from a splice of crispy bacon bits as well.

Inspiration for dishes

- Sautéed Brussels sprouts with bacon, pecan nuts and tossed in cider vinegar
- Fill dumplings with shredded Brussels sprouts and fried bacon bits
- Oven-roasted Brussels sprouts wrapped in pancetta, seasoned with thyme and a squirt of lemon juice

Caramelized onion + Goats cheese

Photo by Caroline Attwood

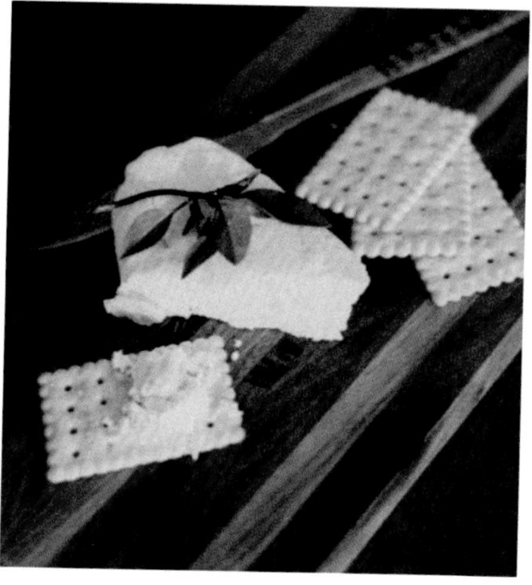

Photo by Anita Peeples

Why it works

The rich and sweet taste of the caramelized onions is enriched further by the aromatic pungent flavor of the goats cheese.

No brainer  Weird

How to prepare

Prepare a rich onion chutney and serve a dollop of it on a cheese-board alongside some goats cheese. You can also incorporate it into dishes – think of hearty and savory baked goods like quiche, tarte tatin, cupcakes or pizza.

Inspiration for dishes

- On a burger with onion chutney and sliced hard goats cheese
- Tarte tatin with shallots, thyme, rosemary and goats cheese
- Savory bacon and onion cupcakes with grilled bell pepper and dollop of soft goats cheese

Sauerkraut + Ham

Photo by Pavlofox

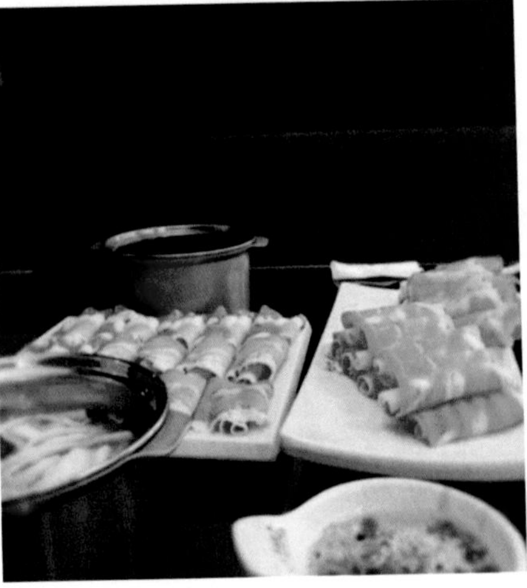

Photo by Esperanza Zhang

No brainer

Weird

Why it works

The saltiness of the ham nicely offsets the sourness and tang of the sauerkraut. Especially mellow versions like cooked ham go really well with the fermented cabbage.

How to prepare

The traditional Polish and German kitchen makes a lot of use of this combination in stews and soups. Diced ham is added to hearty tangy sauerkraut stews and cooked for hours with various spices like cloves and bay leaf.

Inspiration for dishes

- Sauerkraut soup with diced ham and fatty handmade sausage
- Croquettes filled with ham and sauerkraut dipped in remoulade sauce
- Grilled cheese sandwich topped with sliced ham and a tablespoon of sauerkraut

Carrots + Peas

Photo by Jonathan Pielmayer

Photo by Rachael Gorjestani

Why it works

Both carrots and peas have a sweetness as well as a richness to them, especially when cooked fork-tender. The earthiness of the carrots complements the starchy richness of the legumes.

How to prepare

Par-cooked first and then sautéed in butter the two make for a tasty side dish classic. As both can be eaten raw you can also make a salad out of them. Roast the carrots in the oven for some extra caramelized sweetness.

Inspiration for dishes

- Skinny carrot fries with pea puree
- Raw grated carrots with split peas, bacon and a mayo-based vinaigrette
- Roasted carrots with a pea and mint puree

Cauliflower + Curry

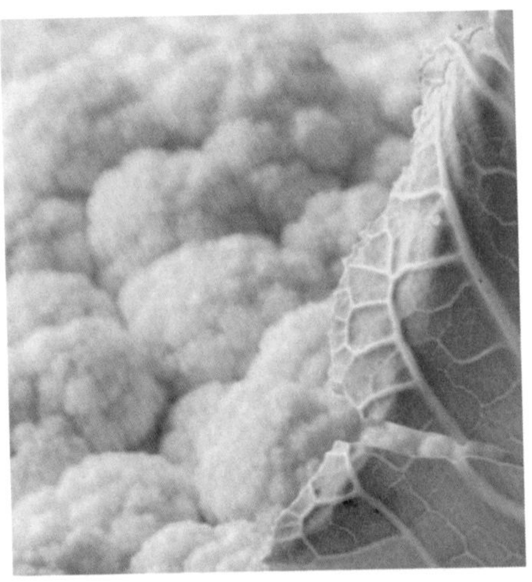

Photo by Engin Akyurt

Photo by Erwan Hesry

Why it works

The sweet earthy bitterness of cauliflower gets an exciting twist when combined with the aromatic Indian spice blend. The cauliflower also takes on the vibrant yellow color extremely well.

No brainer  Weird

How to prepare

The combination with curry power pretty much instantly gives and Indian touch to the dish, regardless if you steam, cook, roast of sauté your cauliflower.

Inspiration for dishes

- Indian pakora fritters: Deep-fried curried cauliflower with cucumber raita dip
- Curry with cauliflower florets, peas and potatoes
- Oven-roasted cauliflower with raisins and almonds

Corn + Lime + Cheese

Photo by Dragne Marius

Photo by Luke Besley

Photo by Anita Peeples

Why it works

Corn itself has a mellow starchy sweet taste, which can be made even richer with some added cheese. The lime on the other hand can cut through the richness, giving the combination a fresh little zing.

No brainer  Weird

How to prepare

'Elotes' are a traditional Mexican street food in which grilled corn on the cob is slathered with mayo, drizzled with mayo and topped with crumbled cojita cheese. Next to serving it on the cob it can be made into a salad, soup of delicious topping for tacos.

Inspiration for dishes

- Elotes - Mexican grilled corn on the cob
- Side salad with cut off cornels, mayo, smoked paprika, cilantro and a spritz of lime
- Vietnamese summer spring rolls filled with corn, shredded cooked chicken, mayo, cheese and cilantro

Dates + Bacon

Photo by Rachael Gorjestani

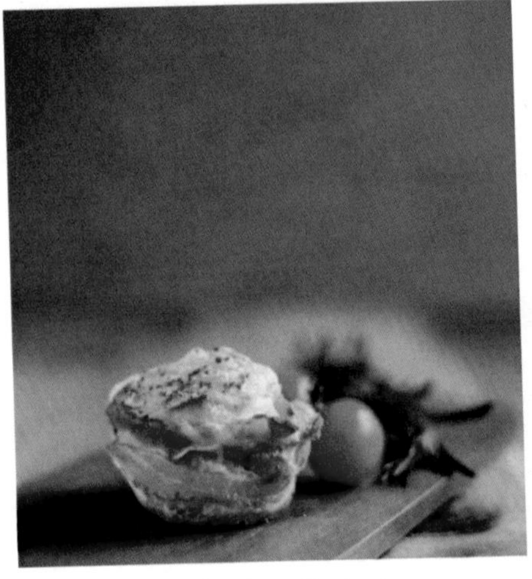

Photo by Margo Brodowicz

Why it works

Another sweet and savory combination in which the creamy sweetness of the dried dates is complemented by the fatty saltiness of the bacon. A rich and decadent treat.

How to prepare

Simply bake bacon-wrapped dates in a pan for a traditional Mediterranean tapas-like bite. You can also chop both up and use them as a delicious filling for various dishes.

Inspiration for dishes

- Dates filled with almonds or cheese, wrapped in bacon and crisped up in a pan
- Quesadillas filled with crispy bacon bits and chopped dates
- Dates stuffed with chorizo and wrapped with bacon
- Have a look at the combination #36 for more inspiration for date dishes

Ham + Cheese

Photo by Petradr

Why it works

Cheese and ham are just two best friends! The saltiness of the ham works perfectly with the rich creaminess of the cheese.

No brainer  Weird

How to prepare

No matter if you put both on a sandwich, on a pizza or use them as delicious filling, this combination is always a winner!

Inspiration for dishes

- Wrap chicory with ham and cheese, then bake in the oven
- Mac & cheese with diced ham
- Grilled cheese sandwich with wholegrain mustard and sliced ham

Fig + Prosciutto

Photo by Matthias Heil

Photo by John Canelis

Why it works

Another sweet savory combination in which the rich saltiness of the cured ham is complemented by the intense sweetness of the figs.

No brainer  Weird

How to prepare

This combination works hot as well as cold. Squash the figs open to expose their sweet flesh and add crumbled baked prosciutto for a delicious salad topping. Or oven-bake figs wrapped in cured ham for a caramelized crispy treat.

Inspiration for dishes

- Oven-baked figs topped with blue cheese, wrapped in prosciutto
- Salad with figs, walnuts, green beans and crispy baked prosciutto
- Pizza spread with fig jam and mozzarella, then topped with cured prosciutto and arugula after baking

Cheese and crackers, with various fruits
Photo by Brooke Lark

Smoked salmon + Horseradish

Photo by Christine Siracusa

Photo by Caroline Attwood

Why it works

The rich fattiness of the smoked salmon gets an extra little kick from the mustard-like pepperiness of the horseradish. The oily fish on the other hand mellows out the rather harsh taste of the radish.

How to prepare

Horseradish makes for a perfect creamy sharp sauce that can be put on- or under the delicious smoky fish. Combine the grated horse-radish with some crème fraiche or crème to mellow it out before using.

Inspiration for dishes

- Oven-roasted potatoes topped with horseradish crème and smoked salmon
- Appetizer: Small little blini pancakes with smoked salmon, dill and lemon juice on horseradish crème
- Cream of horseradish soup topped with smoked salmon, crunchy croutons and dill

Shrimp + Avocado

Photo by Pan Xiaozhen

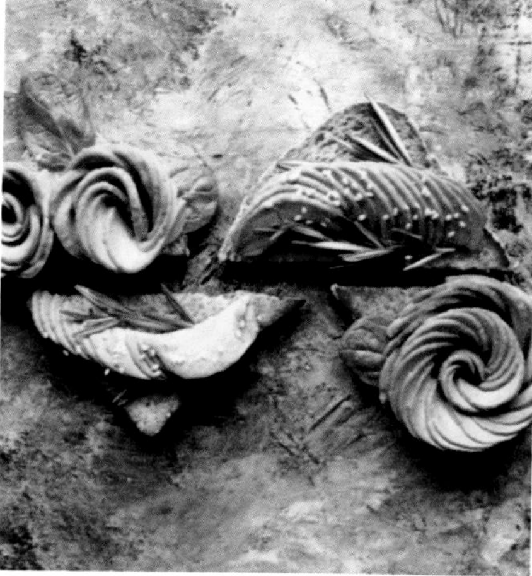

Photo by Brenda Godinez

Why it works

Both avocado and shrimp have quite a subtle flavor profile. The richness of the creamy avocado complements the delicate taste of the shellfish without overpowering it.

No brainer  Weird

How to prepare

Put both on a toast, on a taco, or add cubed avocado to a shrimp ceviche. Make sure other ingredients do not overpower the two! A tiny squirt of lemon or lime juice goes a long way for both of them and brings out their flavor even more.

Inspiration for dishes

- Shrimp ceviche with red onion, cubed avocado and thinly sliced deep-fried plantain chips
- Taco with grilled shrimp and garlicky guacamole
- Salad with steamed shrimp and calamari, tossed in lime, orange, habanero, avocado and cilantro

Apple + Cinnamon

Photo by Roberta Sorge

Photo by Daria Yakovleva

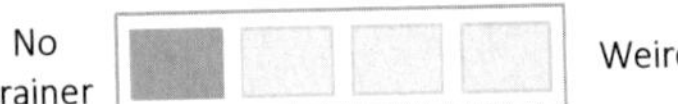

Why it works

The sweetness of the apple gets enriched by the complex sweet spiciness of the cinnamon. Soft apples combined with the slightly burning aromatic cinnamon are just heavenly and automatically make one reminiscent of delicious baked apple pie.

How to prepare

Especially when cooked together the two melt into a rich flavorful sweet combination. Spiced apple compote, sliced apples with a dash of cinnamon or freshly baked apple pie are of course the go-to alternatives.

Inspiration for dishes

- Oat porridge cooked with diced apple and raisins
- Thick crusted apple pie
- Make homemade 'apfelstrudel' inspired liquor

Apple cake with vanilla and cinnamon
Photo by Jean-Marie Leufkens

Bacon + Eggs

Photo by Margo Brodowicz

Photo by Caroline Attwood

No brainer — Weird

Why it works

The eggs need a little salt and the bacon is more than willing to provide that. Crispy smoky bacon and fluffy light scrambled eggs provide very interesting texture contrasts as well.

How to prepare

The two are just the ultimate breakfast treat. Either choose the tried and trusted version and serve them side by side as full English breakfast or incorporate both into a delicious quiche.

Inspiration for dishes

- Scotch eggs: Hardboiled egg with a coating of bacon bits, then deep-fried
- Muffin tray layered with bacon and eggs broken into it; then cooked for individual bacon wrapped cooked eggs
- Quiche Lorraine with bacon, eggs and cheese

Falafel + Tahini

Photo by Brooke Lark

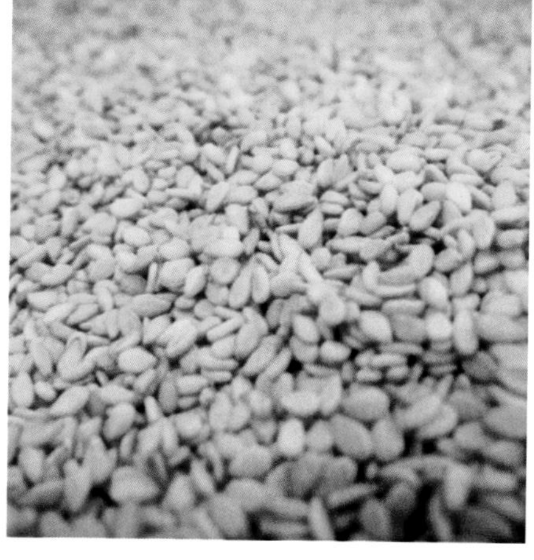
Photo by TheUjulala

Why it works

Crunchy moist falafel loves a rich creamy tahini sauce. Tahini is Middle Eastern sauce made from ground sesame seeds. It gives an interesting texture contrast delivering the perfect base for a variety of sauces and dips.

No brainer  Weird

How to prepare

Blitz up some tahini, chickpeas and garlic for an easy hummus dip for the falafel. Add other interesting flavors to the dipping sauce by incorporating for example mango or carrots into it.

Inspiration for dishes

- Falafel with mango mint hummus
- Falafel burger with lemon tahini sauce and arugula salad
- Meal salad with small falafels, dried tomatoes and tahini yoghurt dressing

Fish + Fennel

Photo by Paul Morris

Photo by Anurag Arora

No brainer ■□□□ Weird

Why it works

Delicate fish fillets do not get overpowered by the subtle anis flavor taste of the fennel. Both have a mellow flavor that melts together into an interesting combination that brings some Mediterranean flair to the table.

How to prepare

You can simmer cubed seafood with fennel in tomato sauce for a delicious stew or use deep-fried fennel on top of a fish fillet makes for an interesting texture contrast. Fennel blended with some cream also makes for a great sauce for grilled fish.

Inspiration for dishes

- Dust sliced fennel in flour and deep-fry it for a crunchy fish topping
- Make a stew with garlic, tomatoes, bell pepper, fennel and cubed fish fillet
- Cream of fennel soup with smoked mackerel

Spinach + Cheese

Photo by Alfonso Cenname

Photo by Jakub Rostkowski

No brainer  Weird

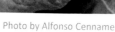

Why it works

The slightly bitter spinach gets extra rich when combined with salty cheese. The salt of the cheese also acts as a seasoning and brings out the flavor of the spinach even more.

How to prepare

Creamed spinach is a delicious ingredient for oven-baked pasta dishes and also works great as a bed for grilled salmon topped with mozzarella. Raw spinach is a tasty green which can be used in salad which then can be topped with crumbled or shaved cheese for extra richness. For a cheesy pizza it is best to blanch the spinach leaves first so they do not burn when baking. Alternatively, just put them on top of your pizza after baking just like you would do with arugula.

Inspiration for dishes

- Spinach soup with pine nuts and Parmesan shavings
- Baked pasta with minced meat, onion, garlic, nutmeg, topped with grated cheese
- Cheese pizza topped with blanched or raw spinach on top

Watermelon + Sea salt

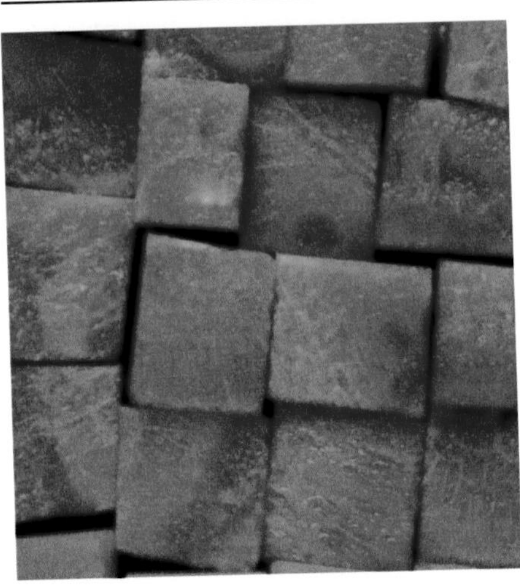

Photo by Joanna Kosinska

Photo by Joel Filipe

No brainer  Weird

Why it works

The fresh sweet summery watermelon taste gets amplified even more when a pinch of sea salt is added to it. The salt also turns the melon into a slightly savory dish.

How to prepare

Simply sprinkle some rough sea salt on top of a slice of watermelon and take a big bite out of it to get to know this delicious combination! Take it a step further and make your watermelon into a cold gazpacho-like soup or turn your watermelon into a delicious fresh salad with a twist.

Inspiration for dishes

- Fresh summer gazpacho with tomato, cucumber and red onion
- Strawberry watermelon smoothie with a pinch of sea salt
- Cubed watermelon with salt, pepper and balsamic vinegar as amuse-gueule
- Have a look at the combination #11 for more watermelon inspiration

Cheese + Honey

Photo by Sonja Langford

Photo by Sonja Langford

Why it works

Rich cheeses in particular can be somewhat overwhelming with their rich and intoxicating taste and smell. The floral notes of the honey with the accompanying sweetness can balance the richness of the cheese and give a little contrast preventing one from getting too saturated from the cheese too quickly.

How to prepare

Different honeys work with different cheeses. On a general level this combinations is always a winning one though. Regardless if pieces of cheese are drizzled with honey or melted cheese is infused with honey, the result will always be rich and indulgent!

Inspiration for dishes

- Panini with melted brie and honey
- Cheeseboard with stilton or goats cheese and a drizzle of honey
- Brie infused with garlic and honey, baked in the oven as dipping bowl

Cheese + Fruit

Photo by Brooke Lark

Why it works

Just like with cheese and honey the sweetness of fruit can complement the cheese and allow for a lot of delicious flavor combination.

No brainer  Weird

How to prepare

Jelly or fruit compote can be used on a cheeseboard or be easily combined on toast, Panini's, or grilled cheese sandwiches.

Inspiration for dishes

- Cheeseboard with different fruit compotes, jams or jellies
- Grilled cheese sandwich with jam
- Sandwich with a smear of strawberry jam and Emmentaler cheese

Photo above by Brooke Lark
Photo on the next page by Orlova Maria

33 daring but delicious combinations

This chapter of the book features the more daring combinations. All these combinations really work, even though you might have your doubts for some of them at first. The general strategies that are working so well in the easy combinations come back here quite often as well. Sweet and savory, acidity cutting through richness, and mellow plus pungent are the extremes that make these unique but interesting combinations so delicious!

A few of these combos are quite common in certain parts of the world, but quite uncommon in others. Take the combination of peanut butter and jelly for example, which is a kids' lunch staple in the US but mostly unheard of in most parts across the pond. Try to keep an open mind and read the description why the ingredients work well together. This is the part of the book that will put your creativity into high gear! Hopefully your first reaction is:

"Well, this sounds a bit strange, but I might just give this a try!"

Chicken + Peanuts

Photo by Idella Maeland

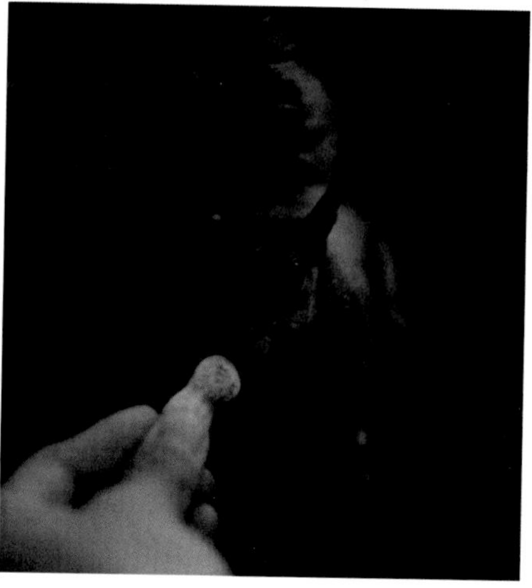

Photo by Jorge Fernandez

Why it works

Delicious grilled chicken skewers get an extra hint of Asian flavor and richness from a spicy peanut sauce. Both melt together into an incredible and indulgent combination.

No brainer 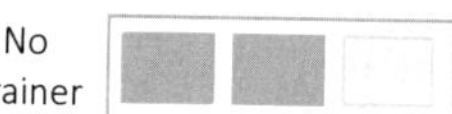 Weird

How to prepare

Make homemade satay peanut sauce from ground peanuts and slather it on grilled chicken skewers. Alternatively make a stew from ground peanuts or peanut butter and simmer diced chicken thighs in it for a rich and creamy delight.

Inspiration for dishes

Quick pad Thai pizza: Cooked chicken and peanut sauce on a tortilla
Steamed fluffy satay chicken filled bao buns
African peanut chicken stew

Chicken + Waffles

Photo by Desiree Fawn

Photo by Pietro de Grandi

Why it works

The crunchy waffle soaks up all the juices from the crispy baked chicken. This not only delivers an interesting texture contrast but also a great sweet and savory flavor combination.

How to prepare

The easiest way to combine the two is to place the fried chicken on top of the crunchy waffle and drizzle both with a glug of maple syrup. You can also put shredded cooked chicken into the waffle batter already. This will make sure that the chicken flavor is truly infused into the waffle.

Recipe ideas by Desmond Gerritse "The Waffle King" // www.ourhangrykitchen.com

Inspiration for dishes

- Surf'n'turf: Fried chicken on a waffle infused with canned tuna and sriracha
- Asian lemongrass chicken waffles
- Fried buttermilk chicken on a waffle topped with maple syrup and bacon bits

Surf 'n' Turf Chicken & Tuna Waffles
Photo and recipe by Desmond Gerritse

Blue cheese + Dates

Photo by Jez Timms

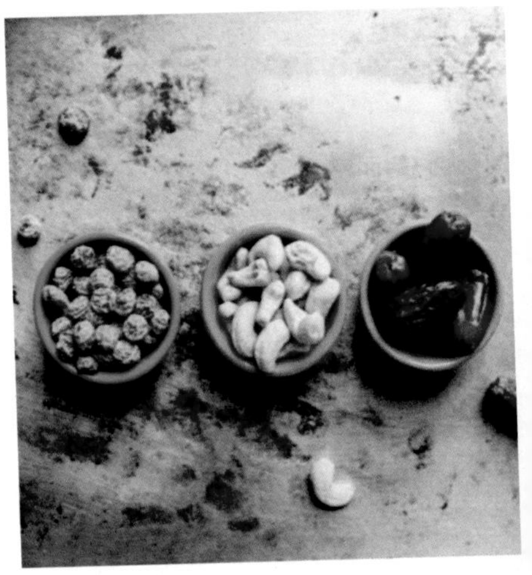

Photo by Rchael Gorjestani

Why it works

The same way that fruit and honey complement cheese in general, the sweet richness of dates works well with blue cheese in particular. The slightly funky taste of the blue cheese is enriched by the sweet creaminess of the dates.

No brainer  Weird

How to prepare

Dates stuffed with blue cheese work especially well, but date products like the Spanish 'pain de datilles' (thick fudgy date nut bread) makes an excellent addition to any cheese board.

Inspiration for dishes

- Quesadilla filled with finely diced dates and clue cheese
- Salad with crumbled blue cheese and chopped dates
- Dates stuffed with blue cheese, wrapped in prosciutto and quickly baked in the oven (see also combination #21)

Sauerkraut + Cheese

Photo by Pavlofox

Photo by Darren Coleshill

No brainer  Weird

Why it works

The tangy and sour flavor of the sauerkraut cuts through the richness and fattiness of the cheese. This will leave you going for another bite and another before the cheese is filling you up.

How to prepare

Sauerkraut is often used as condiment or side-dish but can be easily paired with cheese. Think of the well-known Reuben sandwich which combines gooey melted cheese with tangy sauerkraut. You can also just top your hotdog with both toppings for some extra indulgence. You might even consider a small little snack pile of sauerkraut on a cheeseboard for some extra contrast

Inspiration for dishes

- Small dollop of sauerkraut on a cheeseboard
- Sauerkraut on a grilled cheese sandwich
- Sauerkraut as topping on a pizza

Black olives + Sherry vinegar + Paprika

Photo by Roberta Sorge

Photo by Ashim D'Silva

Photo by Akhil Chandran

Why it works

The sweetness of the sherry vinegar brings out the flavor of the slightly bitter olives. Combined with a dash of smoked paprika you end up with a delicious round little combination.

No brainer  Weird

How to prepare

Given the ingredients are all perfect additions to a lot of dishes, the possibilities are really broad! Salad with cooked meats are a perfect base for them, but you can also make a delicious tapenade out of the three to go on top of grilled meats.

Inspiration for dishes

- Salad with grilled sliced beef, olives and smoky vinaigrette
- Vinegar and paprika marinated chicken, oven-baked in a sauce of tomatoes and black olives
- Tapenade from olives, sherry vinegar and paprika on toasted bread with prosciutto

Butternut squash + Miso

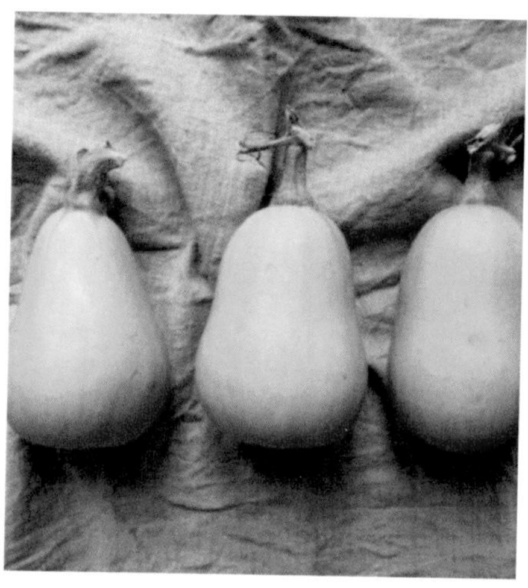

Photo by Gemma Evans

Photo by Henrique Felix

Why it works

The sweet carrot like taste of the squash gets an extreme savory boost from the miso paste. The extra salty umami flavor from the Japanese miso paste enriches the creamy, starchy texture of the pumpkin.

No brainer 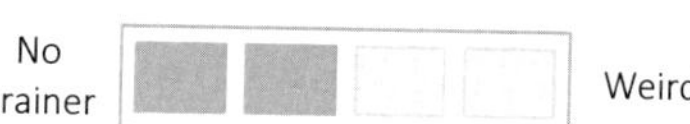 Weird

How to prepare

Miso paste can be used raw in dressings as well making it perfect for roasted butternut squash salad. Both can be blended up into a delicious creamy soup as well.

Inspiration for dishes

- Oven-roasted butternut squash with quinoa and miso dressing
- Pureed butternut squash soup with miso
- Japanese inspired stir-fry with cubed butternut squash, coconut milk, miso and sugar snaps

Carrots + Sugar or Honey

Photo by Gabriel Gurrola

Photo by Roberta Sorge

No brainer  Weird

Why it works

Carrots have a delicate sweetness already which can be brought out even more with the help of some sugar or honey.

How to prepare

Either roast the carrots in the oven or cook them with a pinch of sugar in some water until they are buttery tender.

Inspiration for dishes

- Carrot tarte tatin with honey and thyme
- Fluffy carrot hummus with chickpeas and cardamom
- Oven-roasted carrots with pesto made from carrot greens

Golden-glazed carrot and mushroom tart
Photo by Jean-Marie Leufkens

Peanut butter + Jam or Jelly

Photo by Steve Buissinne

Photo by Monika Grabkowska

No brainer | Weird

Why it works

Beloved lunchbox staple in the US but not as common in the rest of the world. The sticky and slightly salty peanut butter gets a delicious sweet edge from jams, jellies and fruit compotes.

How to prepare

As simple PB&J sandwich or slightly more sophisticated as glaze for chicken and spareribs. Using crushed peanuts instead of creamy peanut butter delivers a great texture contrast.

Inspiration for dishes

- Crunchy peanut butter and grape jelly on a white sandwich
- Oven-baked chicken wings tossed in a peanut butter, raspberry and garlic sauce
- Doritos crusted grilled cheese sandwich with peanut butter and strawberry jam

Steak + Lobster

Photo by Jez Timms

Photo by Francis Macdonald

Why it works

Surf&turf: The best from the earth meets the best of the sea, complementing each other just perfectly. The slightly sweet taste of the lobster gives a light contrast to the rich and slightly fatty steak.

How to prepare

Traditionally side by side (grilled steak and cooked lobster) of course works great, but you can also put both on a bun for the ultimate decadent burger. Most people would consider all combinations of meat and seafood as surf'n'turf though. This makes the possibilities almost endless!

Inspiration for dishes

- Cajun spiced beef strips and shrimps with onion, bell peppers and pasta
- Mini burgers with griddled shrimp, beef patty infused with ginger and garlic, caramelized in sticky oyster sauce
- Salad with beef strips, cooked lobster meat, and tomato-Worcester vinaigrette

Chocolate + Mango

Photo by Michal Grosicki

Photo by Liwanchun

No brainer  Weird

Why it works

The sweet mango gives an exciting twist to the chocolate. Dark chocolate in particular with its extra depth and bitterness profits from the sweetness of the fruit.

How to prepare

A fresh little salsa made from mango aside a rich chocolate dessert makes for interesting taste and texture contrast. Cake with mango loves a swirl of chocolate and a mango compote on top of chocolate ice cream is just exotic and heavenly.

Inspiration for dishes

- Deep-fried, crunchy chocolate and hazelnut spring roll with mango and mint salsa
- Mango shortcake with coconut and dark chocolate shavings
- Chocolate crème brûlée with mango compote and crème fraiche

Cheese + Almond cookies

Photo by Alexander Maasch

Photo by Olenka Kotyk

Why it works

The sweet almond taste of cookies like cantuccini pairs perfectly with the rich flavor of French cheese. It gives a light and sweet contrast to the rich and fatty flavorful cheeses.

No brainer 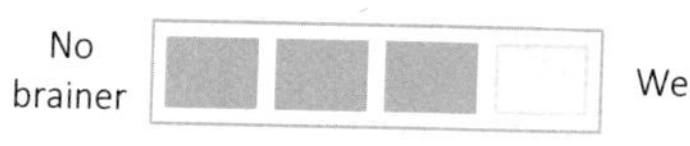 Weird

How to prepare

Combine French cheeses and almond cookies on a cheeseboard to make for a nice closer of a multi-course dinner. All desserts based on fresh cheeses (like ricotta or mascarpone) pair perfectly with the sweet cookies.

Inspiration for dishes

- On a cheeseboard
- Thin cheese wafers made with almond flour, as appetizer or extra texture element
- Cantuccini tiramisu made with mascarpone

Goats cheese + Strawberries

Photo by Anita Peeples

Photo by Clem Onojeghuo

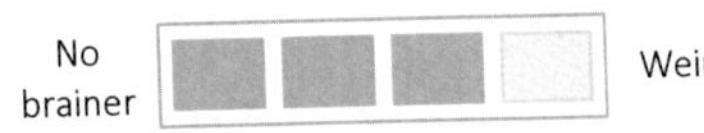

Why it works

The sweet lightly acidic taste of strawberries counterbalances the rich and hearty taste of the goats cheese.

How to prepare

The two can be perfectly paired in a fresh summery salad or be enjoyed on a sandwich. If you use strawberry jam you can put the two together on a cheeseboard as well.

Inspiration for dishes

- On a cheeseboard
- Salad with diced fresh strawberries and dollops of French goats cheese
- Sandwich with sliced fresh strawberries, goats cheese and drizzle of balsamic vinegar

Salami + Grapes

Photo by Alex Guillaume

Photo by Thomas Schaefer

Why it works

The sweetness of the grapes adds to the rich garlicky and sometimes overwhelming taste of the dried salami. Especially the texture contrast from the crunchy fresh grapes and versus the fatty and crumbly or sometimes smearing texture (depending on the type of salami) works counterbalancing and helps to keep the pallet clean.

How to prepare

Of course grapes and sausage make a perfect addition to any cheeseboard, but also on their own they can work great. Think of a sandwich with salami and grape jelly for a tasty salty and sweet combo.

Inspiration for dishes

- On a cheeseboard
- Salami pizza topped with sliced fresh green grapes after baking
- Grilled sandwich topped with salami and grape jelly

Avocado + Chocolate or Cocoa

Photo by Glen Carrie

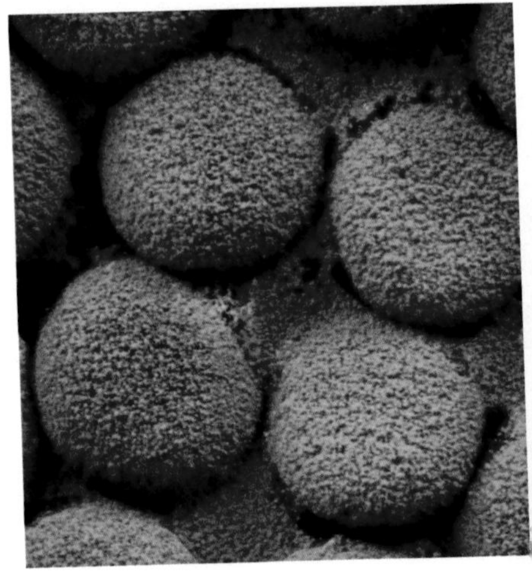

Photo by Michal Kulesza

Why it works

The avocado itself has a very subtle and mellow rich fatty flavor. It takes on the flavor of the cocoa really well, giving you a rich gluten-free and vegan version of chocolate mousse. You will barely notice the avocado.

How to prepare

Mashing and pureeing works best to infuse the two flavors together. Mousses and smoothies turn out great as well.

Inspiration for dishes

- Avocado and chocolate ice cream
- Chocolate truffles made with avocado
- Vegan avocado chocolate mousse
- Have a look at the combination of avocado with vanilla as well (combination #6

Bacon + Banana

Photo by Moerschy

Photo by Mike Dorner

Why it works

The rich smoky bacon lifts the rich intoxicating sweet banana to new heights! This sweet & savory combination just brings out the best in both ingredients.

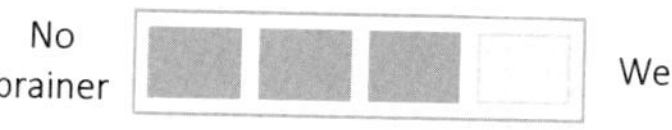

How to prepare

As you can mash up the banana it quite easily it makes for good base of batter in which you can further incorporate the crispy bacon bits. Try various baked goods for some extra crunch!

Inspiration for dishes

- Banana galette with crispy bacon bits
- Banana bacon and vanilla cupcakes
- Grilled sandwich with crispy bacon and sliced banana (see also combination #49)

Banana + Peanuts

Photo by Scott Webb

Photo by Krzysztof Puszczyński

No brainer  Weird

Why it works

The richness of the crunchy peanuts offers a great texture contrast to the sweet mushy banana. Especially when salted peanuts are used the saltiness brings out the sweet flavor of the bananas even more.

How to prepare

Whole toasted peanuts can be easily crushed and sprinkled on top of dishes. Creamy peanut butter works especially well when blended together with mushed-up bananas. Use both ingredients also as basis for baked goods like cupcakes or muffins.

Inspiration for dishes

- (N)ice-cream: Simple ice-cream made from frozen bananas and peanut butter
- Banana split with crushed salty peanuts
- Grilled sandwich with peanut butter, crispy bacon and sliced banana - Allegedly one of Elvis Presley's favorites (see also combination #48)

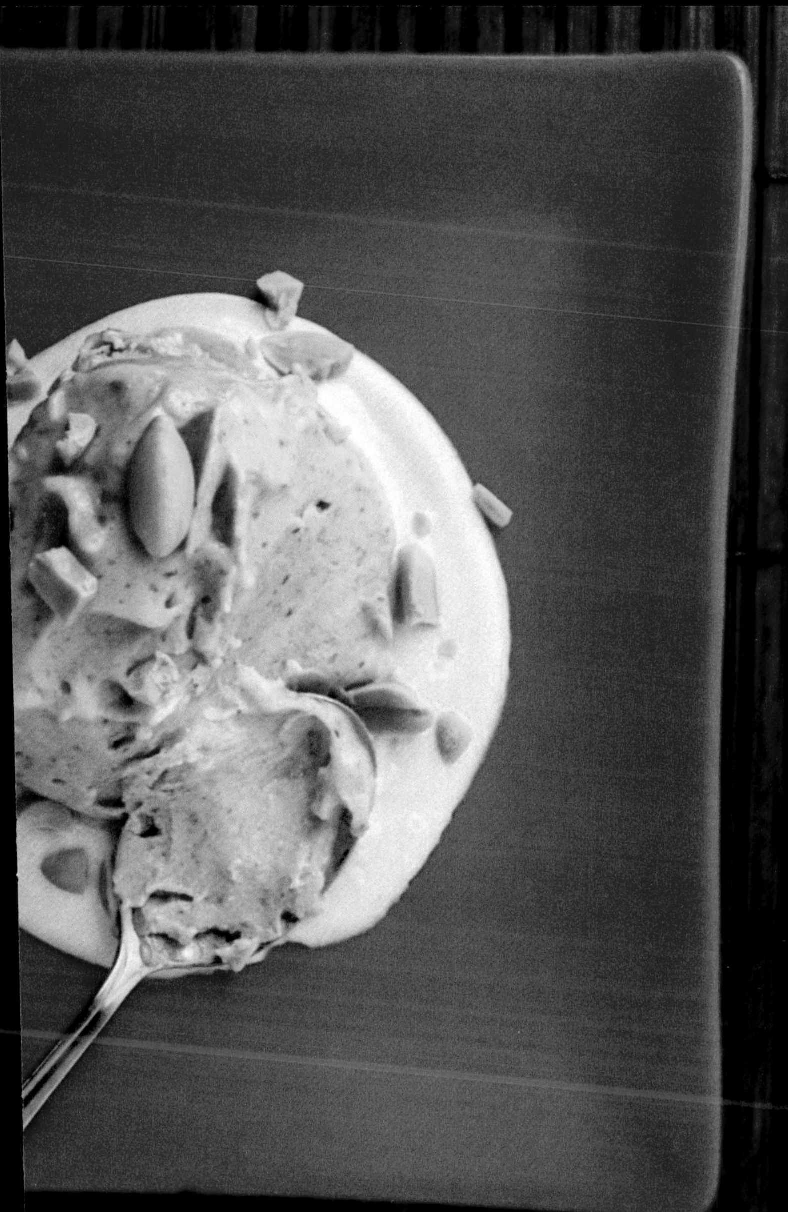

Banana + Sesame

Photo by Alice Young

Photo by TheUjulala

Why it works

The toasty subtle flavor of sesame goes great with the sweet rich flavor of the banana and gives it some extra depth.

No brainer  Weird

How to prepare

Toasted sesame seeds can easily be sprinkled on top of all banana dishes. Another nice way is to incorporate both into a batter. A shortcut here is to use tahini paste, which is a Middle Eastern paste from ground sesame seeds which reminds one of runny peanut butter.

Inspiration for dishes

- Deep-fried banana sprinkled with sesame seeds and drizzled with honey
- Banana split with a drizzle of tahini and honey
- Yoghurt with diced banana and sesame granola

Chicken + Apple (sauce)

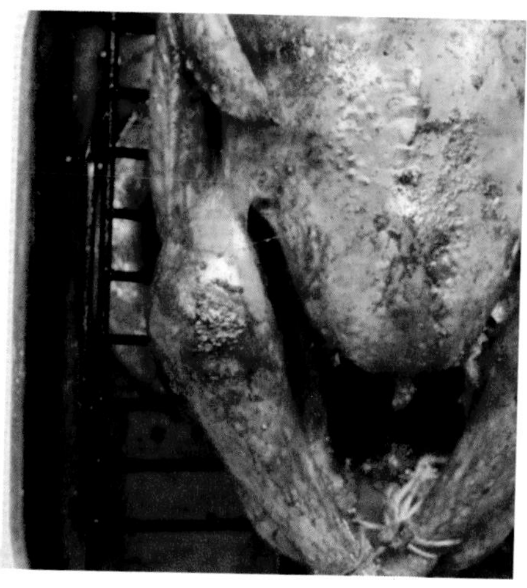

Photo by Alison Marras

Photo by Roberta Sorge

Why it works

Succulent chicken gets and extra boost of flavor from sweet cooked apple compote. Especially when tangy apples are used this cuts through the richness of the chicken.

How to prepare

Rotisserie chicken with fries and apple compote is a Dutch comfort treat classic. A piece of grilled chicken with an apple relish is a slightly more refined version. Diced chicken and sour apple also make an awesome addition to a light salad.

Inspiration for dishes

- Roasted chicken with apple sauce and fries
- Grilled chicken with apple, thyme and onion relish
- Green salad with diced chicken, apples and honey-mustard vinaigrette

Chicken + Cherries

Photo by Paulo Morales

Photo by Michal Grosicki

No brainer

Weird

Why it works

Chicken tastes great with the addition of fresh juicy fruit. Tart cherries are of course no exception. The sourness of the cherries cuts through the richness of the chicken and delivers a sweet note.

How to prepare

The cherries can of course be used whole or cooked-down into compote. Cherry sauce, compote and jam on top of grilled chicken is just delicious. Both ingredients work perfectly as a filling for a quiche or samosas as well.

Inspiration for dishes

- Cherry jam glazed chicken, baked in the oven
- Samosas with cherries, ginger, curry and chicken filling
- Salad with shredded chicken and a cherry jam vinaigrette

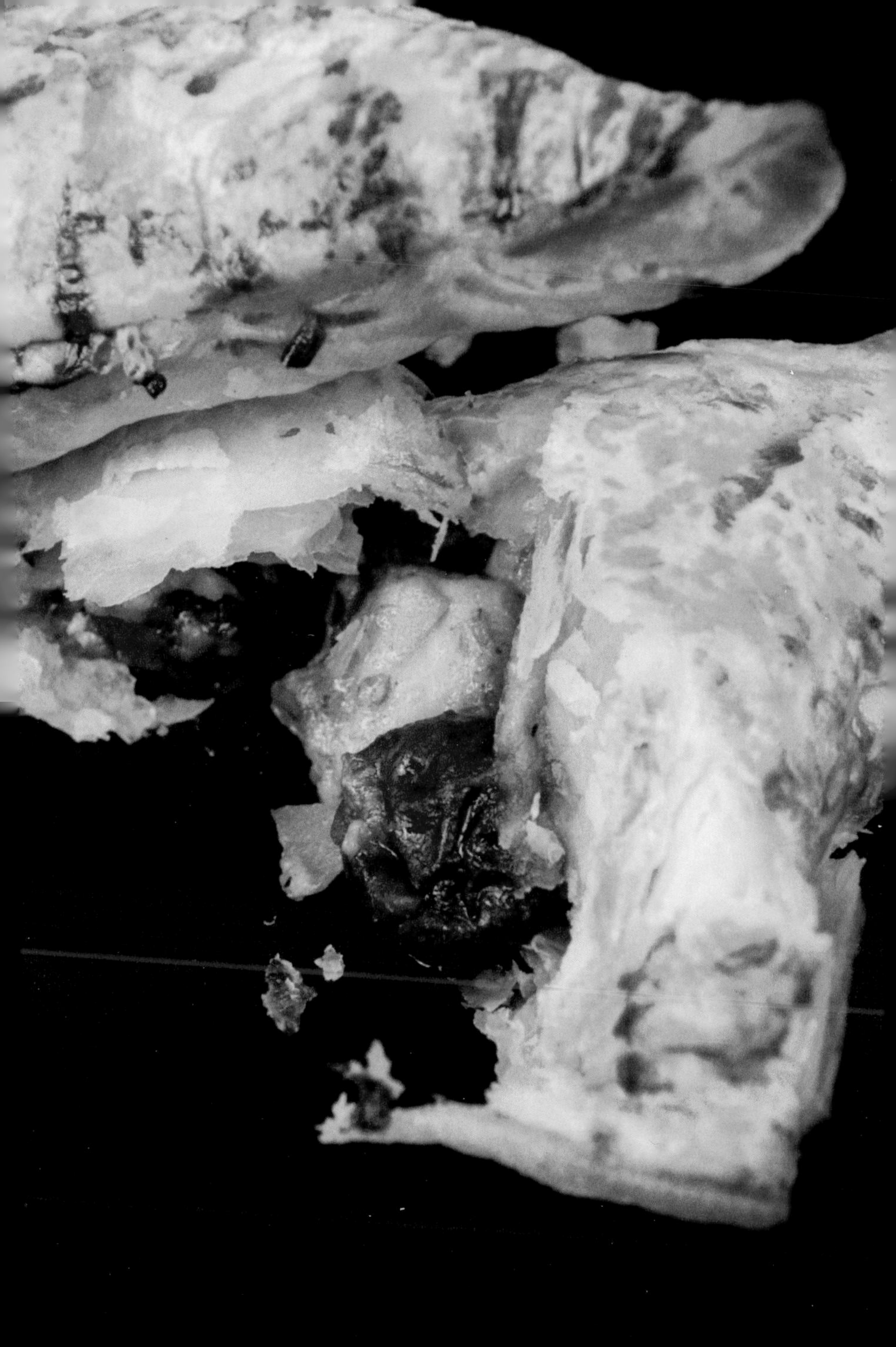

Baked chicken, cherry and ginger samosa
Photo by Jean-Marie Leufkens

Fish + Mango

Photo by Caroline Attwood

Photo by Luhaifeng

No brainer  Weird

Why it works

Delicate sea food gets and exotic punch from tangy mango, especially when the mango is not fully ripe and overwhelmingly sweet yet. The slight sourness of the mango brings out the fish flavor just like lime or lemon juice normally would.

How to prepare

Create a delicious easy mango salsa as topping for your fish dishes. You can also bake fish fillets in the oven in a mango cream sauce. Even when combined with raw fish fillet in a ceviche, the mango gives and incredible contrast to the fish.

Inspiration for dishes

- Fish tacos with mango and cabbage slaw
- Ceviche from white fish, red onion and cubed mango
- Fish and mango curry with garlic, ginger and coconut milk

French fries + Pickles

Photo by Hans Vivek

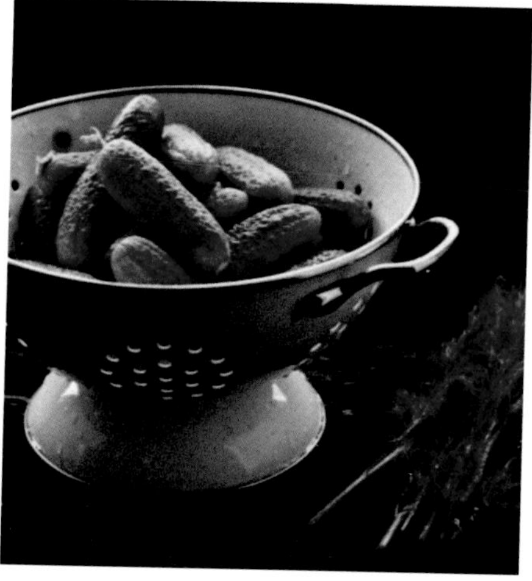

Photo by Jonathan Pielmayer

Why it works

There is a reason why you always find those slices pickles on your burgers. The tangy pickles cut through the richness of the fat, making the dish slightly lighter, more interesting and cleaning your palette. The same also works for your French fries!

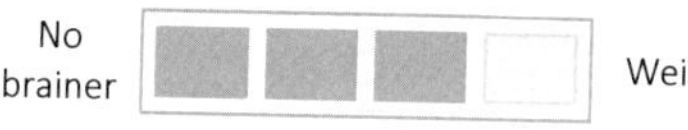

How to prepare

French fries are French fries, but this combination works with all fried potato side dishes like latkes, röstis, potato wedges and even baked potatoes. Either just add sliced pickles to the dishes or create a quick relish from diced gherkins.

Inspiration for dishes

- Gherkin sauce with sour cream and capers as dipping sauce for fries
- Bread roll with fries and sliced gherkins
- Fries and fried dill pickles as sides for burgers

Pepperoni + Sauerkraut

Photo by Torsten Dettlaff

Photo by Pavlofox

Why it works

Smoked, dried garlicky sausage goes so well with sauerkraut. The tartness of the sauerkraut cuts through the richness of the heavy dense sausage making the dish lighter. When frying the sliced sausage the fat leaks out. This rendered fat can be used to cook the fermented cabbage, delivering extra depth and complexity.

How to prepare

Put dollops of sauerkraut on pepperoni pizza as delicious topping or go the other way around and put crispy fried chorizo on top of your sauerkraut stew. If you simmer cured sausage, sauerkraut and potatoes all the flavors will truly melt together.

Inspiration for dishes

- Grated potato and sauerkraut latkes topped with tomato-chorizo relish
- Pepperoni pizza with sauerkraut
- Sauerkraut stew with crispy chorizo and Parmesan crackers

Peanut butter + Sambal

Photo by Steve Buissinne

Photo by Elli O.

No brainer  Weird

Why it works

Fatty roasted nuts can always profit from some extra spice! Different types of sambal can give a delicious spicy twist to the sometimes ordinary nuts. Creamy peanut butter is the perfect base to take on additional flavors. As sambal is usually slightly salty as well, you can use unsalted peanuts or nut butter.

How to prepare

Spiced sauce from ground peanuts, also known as satay or saté works incredibly with grilled chicken and is a traditional staple in the Indonesian and Thai kitchen. You can save time and effort by simply combining peanut butter and sambal on a sandwich. Different types of sambal will give you different levels of heat and flavor nuances. Instead of peanuts you can also use other nuts like cashews.

Inspiration for dishes

- Spicy satay sauce on grilled chicken skewers
- Hamburger with chicken, garlic, ginger and a dollop of satay sauce
- Roasted cashews with sambal coating

Tuna + Sesame

Photo by Taylor Grote

Photo by Pezibear

No brainer  Weird

Why it works

Oily rich tuna gets and extra boost of flavor from the aromatic and slightly bitter sesame. Especially when you use tahini sauce and raw tuna their creaminess just melts together in your mouth.

How to prepare

Canned tuna and tuna steak have very different flavors offering various possibilities for the combination with sesame in its different forms. Combine canned tuna with a drizzle of sesame oil and fish sauce for a quick Asian twist in a salad. Coat tuna steaks with sesame seeds before baking for a delicious crust. Or combine cubed raw tuna with tahini for a delicious poke – either as side dish for sushi or as topping for a sushi bowl.

Inspiration for dishes

- Cesar's salad with Asian dressing from lime juice, sesame oil and fried shallots
- Tuna poke with scallions and jalapeno
- Sesame seared tuna steak on a salad

Creamy sesame tuna poke with jalapeños
Photo by Jean-Marie Leufkens

Stout beer + Chocolate

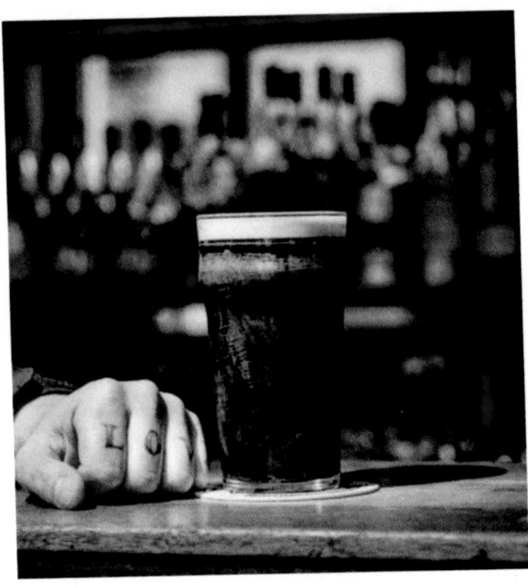

Photo by Oliver Wendel

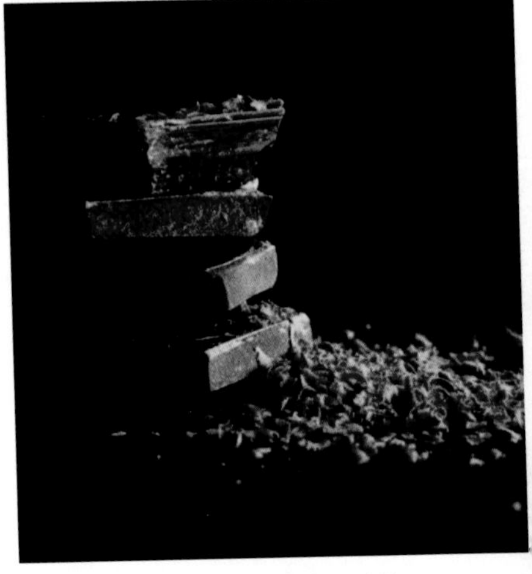

Photo by Michal Grosicki

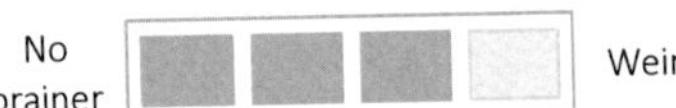

Why it works

Stout beers like Guinness often have notes of chocolate in them already. This can be further enhanced with actual chocolate. The result will be a deeply complex mix of flavors which will heavily depend on the cocoa content of your chocolate as well on the variety stout beer you use.

How to prepare

The two can of course be combined in a sauce that is a perfect topping for ice creams or other desserts. If you go one step further you can incorporate both into various baked goods like cakes or muffins. The stout makes your cakes fudgy, moist and adds a different level of richness without being fatty.

Inspiration for dishes

- Glazed chocolate and stout muffins
- Brownie Sundaes with warm chocolate stout sauce
- Chocolate stout gelato

Nutella + Soft cheese

Photo by Brenda Godinez

Photo by Jez Timms

Why it works

The rich sweet hazelnut spread melts together with the strong aromatic and creamy cheese into sweet pungent perfection.

No brainer 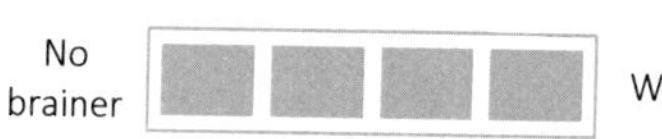 Weird

How to prepare

The easiest way to marry the two is by combining them on a warm bread roll or grilled cheese sandwich. Another interesting way is to deconstruct the flavors of Nutella and use chopped hazelnuts and dark chocolate instead of the branded hazelnut spread.

Inspiration for dishes

- Grilled cheese sandwich with Nutella
- Bread roll with Nutella and brie
- Pasta with brie sauce, crushed hazelnuts and dark chocolate shavings
- Look at the combination #64 for more inspiration on cheese with chocolate

Bacon + Chocolate

Photo by Gabriel Gurrola

Photo by Cala

No brainer 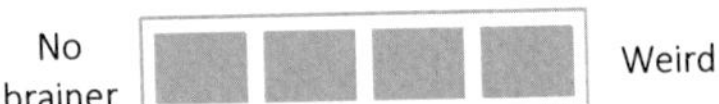 Weird

Why it works

This combination sounds odd at first but the salt from the bacon brings out the taste of the chocolate even more (think of salted caramel!). Because both are rich and quite fatty, the flavors just melt together beautifully.

How to prepare

Try it as traditional state-fair novelty food in the form of chocolate covered bacon on a stick. Of course you can incorporate both into baked goods or give your chocolate treats a little sprinkle with roasted bacon crumbs.

Inspiration for dishes

- Crispy bacon on a stick covered with chocolate
- 's mores with crispy bacon
- Chocolate cupcakes with crunchy bacon sprinkle

Bourbon + Pickle juice

Photo by Michael Mroczek

Photo by Photo-Mix

Why it works

The smoky harsh bourbon taste is completely neutralized by the sour spicy pickle juice. Both have a deep rich complex flavor at completely opposite sides of the flavor spectrum, making for an amazing and interesting contrast.

No brainer  Weird

How to prepare

Try a "Pickle back" which is shot of bourbon immediately followed by a shot of pickle juice that works as an amazing palette cleanser. Of course you can incorporate it into dishes as well, especially because pickle juice makes for an amazing chicken marinade.

Inspiration for dishes

- Pickle back: A shot of bourbon followed by a shot of pickle juice
- Chicken marinated in pickle juice, roasted in the oven with bourbon bacon sauce
- Salad with finely diced gherkin pickles and bacon Dijon vinaigrette

Red cabbage + Raisin bread

Photo by Chuttersnap

Photo by Jennifer Pallian

Why it works

The peppery earthy and slightly bitter cabbage gets a lift from the sweetness of the raisin bread. The fluffy white bread also sucks up all flavors the cooked cabbage releases.

No brainer 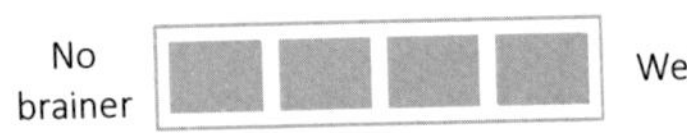 Weird

How to prepare

The soft raisin bread gets especially delicious when toasted to crunchy perfection. The cabbage gets mellower when cooked until soft. Caramelize the red cabbage in some honey or sugar to mellow out the flavor even more.

Inspiration for dishes

- Caramelized red cabbage on raisin bread French toast
- Red cabbage slaw with raisin bread croutons
- Cabbage bread pudding made with raisin bread

Chicken + Cola

Photo by Jairo Alzate

Photo by Francesco Gallarotti

Why it works

Adding soda to a piece of poultry sounds like a weird idea but the sweetness from the cola enriches the chicken and gives it an interesting little twist, especially when caramelized.

No brainer

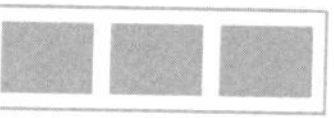

Weird

How to prepare

The soft drink can be used either as glaze or marinate for the chicken. Put both into a slow cooker for tender succulent and easy pulled chicken.

Inspiration for dishes

- Grilled chicken with cola barbecue sauce
- Slow cooked chicken made with Dr. Pepper; shredded on a sandwich
- Chicken drumsticks marinated in cola, garlic, ketchup, and red pepper; then grilled

Chocolate + Cheese

Photo by Nordwood Themes

Photo by Damien Kuhn

Why it works

Rich complex dark chocolate pairs really well with salty mature cheeses. It's an amazing sweet savory combination in which the saltiness and umami brings out the flavor of the chocolate even more. You will also be amazed how well a chocolate spread like Nutella will go together with rich creamy cheeses like brie or camembert.

No brainer  Weird

How to prepare

Of course a sandwich is the easiest way to combine the two. Fresh cheeses embrace chocolate for delicious chocolate-infused cheesecakes. Shavings of white chocolate on a cheese pizza makes for ultimate sweet and savory decadence.

Inspiration for dishes

- Simple cheese pizza without tomato sauce and shavings of white chocolate
- Grilled cheese sandwich with brie, dark chocolate and raspberries
- Sandwich with Edam cheese and chocolate spread
- Have a look at combination #59 for other dishes with brie and chocolate spre

Raisin bread + Cheese

Photo by Jennifer Pallian

Photo by Alice Donovan Rouse

Why it works

Grapes on a cheeseboard are definitely a no-brainer, but what about dried grapes - or in other words: raisins? Just like grapes would, the raisins add sweetness to the salty cheese. Raisins engulfed in sweetened bread are the perfect base to add cheese onto.

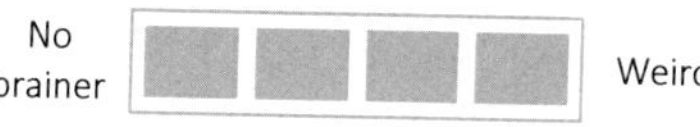

How to prepare

Toast some raisin bread for an extra delicious crust that almost tastes like cake. Dice up some toasted raisin bread and skewer with a small cube of cheese for an easy amuse-gueule. An easy sandwich made from raisin bread with sliced cheese works of course as well.

Inspiration for dishes

- Green salad with raisin bread croutons and shaved Parmesan cheese
- Sandwich from raisin bread, Nutella and brie (see also combinations #59 & #64)
- Grilled cheese from raisin bread with Edam cheese

Avocado + Vanilla

Photo by Glen Carrie

Photo by Cel Lisboa

Why it works

Most people in the Western world associate avocado with something savory, but on it's own the fatty fruit does not have much flavor to begin with. This makes it the perfect base to take on additional flavor. Vanilla adds a comforting cozy flavor to the avocado and makes for a spectacular combination. The rich and complex flavor of the vanilla practically melts into the subtle avocado.

No brainer  Weird

How to prepare

As avocado has a very creamy texture it makes for a healthy vegan substitute for cream or butter. Use vanilla or vanilla extract in pureed avocado as cake frosting, basis for shakes and smoothies as well as pudding.

Inspiration for dishes

- Vegan smoothie with coconut milk and banana
- (n)ice cream with banana and maple syrup
- Make cake frosting with confectioners sugar and lemon juice
- Also have a look at the combination of avocado with chocolate (#47)

Wine and cheese in Paris
Photo by John Canelis

An extraordinary cheeseboard

What makes a good cheeseboard?

There are a few basic principles that every proper cheeseboard should follow – you want variation in your cheeses, but on top you want your guests to taste the cheeses in a certain sequence. That way they can fully appreciate the different cheese flavors.

In terms of variation for your cheeses you want something...

- **...creamy** (e.g. brie or camembert)
- **...fresh** (e.g. un-aged cheeses like mozzarella or goats cheese)
- **...sharp** (e.g. aged Cheddar)
- **...nutty** (e.g. smoked Gouda, Gruyere or Manchego)
- ...and **funky** (e.g. blue cheeses like Gorgonzola or Roquefort)

Your guests will also appreciate it, if the cheeses come from different animal milks. Meaning, you want cheeses made from cows milk, but also from goats and sheep.

The order in which you want to eat the cheeses is from soft to harder, but always ending with the blue cheese. To make it easier for your guest, just place the cheeses in the order they should be eating them. Start with the soft cheese on top of your board and simply go clockwise.

Also, always make sure you serve your cheeses at room temperate so they can share all their flavor! Better get them out of the fridge about an hour before serving.

Now let's make it extraordinary!

If you really want to impress your guests with your cheeseboard you need to go a few steps further than just having cheese. Add different texture elements, a few palate cleansers as well as some unexpected flavor combinations to complement your cheeses!

Neutral crackers are okay, but go one step further and dare to serve some almond cookies too (flavor combination #44) for a sweet light contrast. Another interesting twist is using toasted raisin bread (#65) as crunchy addition.

Fruit in all forms (#33) not only adds color but also sweetness and a little zing to your cheeseboard. Blue cheese pairs particularly well with dates (#36), whereas goats cheese loves strawberries (#45). To add some extra sweetness drizzle some of your cheeses with a little honey (#32). For the slightly more adventurous dare to add a small dollop of Nutella next to your brie or camembert (#59). Delicious!

A little sourness can cut through the overwhelming richness of the cheeses. What about adding a tiny pile of sauerkraut (#37) to your board to add that little extra zing?

Cured meats make for a great addition as well. Did you know they pair well with grapes? (#46)

Cheese platter with delicious combinations
Photo by Jean-Marie Leufkens

Who took most of the delicious photos?

A big thank you to the Unsplash.com community!

Most photos in this book were submitted to websites that make them available completely for free. I want to thank all the selfless and altruistic authors one by one, with the whole Unsplash community in particular. Some photos were gathered from other sites as well. These are credited on the right. Please join me in thanking all the generous photographing artists featured!

Featured photographers from Unsplash.com

Akhil Chandran
Alex Guillaume
Alexander Maasch
Alfonso Cenname
Alice Young
Alice Donovan
Alison Marras
Andrew Ridley
Anita Peeples
Anurag Arora
Ashim D. Silva
Ashwin Vaswani
Beth Teutschmann
Brenda Godinez
Brooke Lark
Cala
Caroline Attwood
Cel Lisboa
Christine Siracusa
Clem Onojeghuo
Damien Kuhn
Darren Coleshill
Dave Meier
Dennis Klein
Desiree Fawn
Dominik Martin
Dragne Marius
Elli O
Engin Akyurt
Erwan Hesry
Esperanza Zhang
FireskyStudios.com
Francesco Gallarotti
Francis MacDonald
Gabriel Gurrola
Gemma Evans
Glen Carrie
Hans Vivek
Henrique Felix
Hoach Le Dinh
Idella Maeland
Jairo Alzate
Jakub Kapusnak
Jay Wennington
Jennifer Pallian
Jez Timms
Joanna Kosinska
Joel Filipe
John Canelis
Jonathan Pielmayer
Jorge Gonzalez
Jorge Fernandez
Katerina Pavlickova
Keenan Loo
Krista McPhee
Luke Besley
Margo Brodowicz
Matthias Heil
Michael Mroczek
Michal Grosicki
Mike Dorner
Monika Grabkowska
Nabil Boukala
Neha Deshmukh
Nick Grappone
Nordwood Themes
Olenka Kotyk
Oliver Wendel
Orlova Maria
Pan Xiaozhen
Paul Morris
Paulo Morales
Pietro de Grandi
Pitor Lohunko
Rachael Gorjestani
Roberta Sorge
Scott Webb
Sonja Langford
Syd Wachs
Taylor Grote
Thomas Shaefer
Thomas Rehehauser

Featured photographers from pxhere.com & pixabay.com

Chuttersnap
CongerDesign
Coyot
Daria
Erbs55
Jakub
Jenniger Pallian
Krzysztof Puszczynski
Liwanchun
LuhaiFeng279
Michal
Moerschy
Pavlofox
Petradr
Pezibear
Photo Mix
Steve Buisinne
TheUjulala
Tookapic
Torsten Dettlaff

Waffle photo on page 61 was taken b
Desmond Gerritse a.k.a. "The Waffle King
You can find his internationally feature
recipes on www.ourhangrykitchen.com

Big thank you to the talented photographers!
Photo by Brooke Lark

A big thank you to Sanne!

Thank you Sanne for your time and feedback on this book

At this point I would really like to thank Sanne Ursem for her help on this book! Thank you for the time and effort on co-reading this book in your spare time while juggling your busy personal and professional life. Your knowledge, input and feedback are deeply appreciated and made this book better than it originally was!

Sanne and her hidden alter-ego

Sanne has a background in anthropology and likes to fully immerse herself in every topic she touches. The Dutch food blogger world is small and as fate has it Sanne and myself ended up in the same market research company even though in slightly different departments.

When she introduced herself as Sanne I of course had no idea about her alter-ego SesuChops. It actually took a few weeks until another colleague of ours mentioned to me that Sanne has a food blog as well.

At that point everything made a lot more sense and ever since then we obviously chit-chat about food, photography and recipes on a regular basis. We are both lucky to work for a lot of food related clients as well, which makes combining the day-job with our both passion a lot easier.

A deep love for food and beer

Sanne creates amazing Dutch-Korean fusion recipes for her foodblog www.SesuChops.nl. Her creations as well as mouthwatering photos got featured on several national and internal food sites like the feedfeed.com. Even before we met in person several of her recipes ended up on my culinary to-do list.

Sanne also loves to spread the tasty fizzy beverages of talented local Dutch craft beer brewers on her platform HopperBier.nl. Together with her boyfriend they travel the country to interview the nations best and innovative brewers.

I was lucky enough to be collab-orate with her on the bloggers-choice box where the favorite beers of several bloggers ended up in one of the monthly subscription beer boxes that get delivered right to your doorstep. If you love bee and want to try some extra ordinary brews in the comfort c your own home, why not give it go?

SESU
CHOPS

Sanne juggling food and beers!
Photos by Jaap Vork. © Hopper Bierbox

Who wrote this book and why?

Jean-Marie " Johnny" Leufkens

Hi, my name is Johnny, I started cooking when I was about 18 and fell in love with food ever since. Truth be told, I'm not a professional or trained chef, but I have a deep passion for everything that is related to food.

I studied marketing and my research about the fear of novel and unknown foods ended up in the scientific literature. Currently I work in market research for mostly big international food companies where I help them to find the next big product! In my spare time I love to write recipes and take pictures of food. My first book "In Johnny's Kitchen" was published end of August 2017 and is available worldwide through Amazon. Next to that, I have written guest posts for several food related websites and regularly publish recipes on my website.

My deep passion for food drives me to push the envelope and challenge the existing beaten paths in the cooking- and restaurant business.

Understanding flavor

Being a hobby chef I am always searching for new recipes and flavor combinations. When I stumbled across IBM's 'ChefWatson' I was immediately hooked! The artificial intelligence creates recipes based on the chemical make-up of ingredients, resulting in endless possibilities.

Hours of reading online posts, scientific articles and books on the topic just fueled my interest even more. Especially the difference in culture on how to combine flavors was so interesting to me. I spent countless hours in the kitchen trying the weirdest of the weirdest combinations to see if these would actually work together. The more I understood individual flavors, the more my skills as chef developed. As I truly believe in the power of sharing knowledge, I wanted to save you the countless hours of desk-research and let you start cooking right away. For you and me these are only the first steps of a never-ending delicious journey!

www.injohnnyskitchen.com and www.linkedin.com/in/jeanmarieleufkens

Yup, that's me...
Photo by Erwin Spil

Index by combination

Two different indexes to make your life easier

To make it easier for you to find the combination you are looking for you will find two kinds of indexes on the following pages. One index by the number (indicated with #) as seen on the top right of each combination. This index is quick overview of all the combinations. The second index starting on page 101 is sorted by ingredients. This way you can start with one ingredient and look for relevant combos.

The more classic, tried and trusted combinations

#1 Anchovies + parsley

#2 Fish sauce + lime juice + brown sugar

#3 Ginger + garlic + spring onion

#4 Bacon + maple syrup

#5 Cumin + oregano + chipotle

#6 Honey + mustard

#7 Cilantro + lime

#8 Mushrooms + tarragon + crème fraiche or cream

#9 Prosciutto + melon

#10 Tomato + basil

#11 Watermelon + feta and + mint

#12 Yoghurt + cucumber + dill

#13 Broccoli + garlic

#14 Banana + chocolate

#15 Brussels sprouts + bacon

#16 Caramelized onion + goats cheese

#17 Sauerkraut + ham

#18 Carrots + peas

#19 Cauliflower + curry

#20 Corn + lime + cheese

#21 Dates + Bacon

#22 Ham + cheese

#23 Fig + prosciutto

#24 Smoked salmon + horseradish

#25 Shrimp + avocado

#26 Apple + cinnamon

#27 Bacon + eggs

#28 Falafel + tahini

#29 Fish + fennel

#30 Spinach + cheese

#31 Watermelon + sea salt

#32 Cheese + honey

#33 Cheese + fruit

Index by combination # - continued

The more daring but delicious combinations

Notes and own combinations

Index by ingredient

Overview of all the combinations sorted by ingredients

Index by ingredient - continued

Overview of all the combinations sorted by ingredients

Notes and own combinations

Made in the USA
Lexington, KY
27 October 2018